THE ATOMIC TIMES

THE
ATOMIC
TIMES

*My H-Bomb Year
at the Pacific
Proving Ground*

A MEMOIR

MICHAEL HARRIS

BALLANTINE BOOKS
NEW YORK

Published in the United States by Presidio Press, an imprint of The Random House Publishing Group, a division of Random House, Inc., New York.

PRESIDIO PRESS and colophon are trademarks of Random House, Inc.

Library of Congress Cataloging-in-Publication Data

Harris, Michael (Michael David)
The atomic times: my H-bomb year at the Pacific Proving Ground / Michael Harris.
p. cm.
ISBN 0-345-48154-2
1. Harris, Michael (Michael David)   2. United States. Army—Military police—Biography.   3. Nuclear weapons—Testing.   4. Enewetak Atoll (Marshall Islands)—History, Military.   5. Eniwetok Proving Grounds (Marshall Islands)   I. Title.
U53.H33.A3 2005
355.8'25119'0973—dc22
[B]   2005043149

Printed in the United States of America on acid-free paper

www.presidiopress.com

2   4   6   8   9   7   5   3   1

First Edition

Book design by Susan Turner

For Ruth:
Love at first instant and every instant after
And that's just for openers

The Atomic Times *is dedicated to the men of Operation Redwing—
and to all the other Atomic Veterans. They fought an invisible enemy and
displayed a kind of bravery not required of American servicemen before or
since.*

This book is for those who managed to survive.
And for those who didn't.

ACKNOWLEDGMENTS

I want to particularly thank the many Eniwetok veterans who remembered and helped—especially Leon Nelms, Chuck Morgan, Bob Cherouny and Wayne Parsons.

At Random House/Ballantine/Presidio: Many thanks to Nancy Miller, for getting the book into the right hands. To Ron Doering, whose hands they were, for his support and encouragement from day one. Tim Mak, for his help, enthusiasm and hard work. Thanks also to Susan Turner, Nancy Delia, Carl Galian, Grant Neumann, Dean Curtis, Claire Tisne and Amelia Zalcman, whose skill and care helped bring the book to life. To Kate Medina for her efforts. To publicists Lisa Barnes, Brian McLendon and Tom Perry for theirs.

Also, in the Support-and-Encouragement Department, my very special friends: Patti Harris, Bob McKelvey, Barry Theiler, William Machado and Dr. Henry Erle. And, of course, the crucial cheering section of Nippy and Anna (for decades) and (more recently) John.

My deep appreciation to Molly Friedrich, the first person (besides Ruth) to believe in *The Atomic Times*, and to her colleagues Paul Cirone and Frances Jalet-Miller—upping the early-believer total from one to four.

Thanks to Michael Brandman and Keith Whittle for their help and to Frank Curtis for his—present and past.

To Philip Schwartzberg, Meridian Mapping, Minneapolis, for his maps.

And, of course, the Queen of the Clipboard. Without whom . . .

CONTENTS

AUTHOR'S NOTE

I have given fictional names to all the men on Eniwetok I write about (with the exception of Bo Goldman). Any similarity to actual individuals is unintentional and coincidental.

Some men are described as they were.

Sometimes I made changes in their backgrounds and in their personal and physical characteristics to conceal identities and preserve privacy.

Sometimes I combined characters for the same reasons.

But all the men are real people, and much of their dialogue is authentic.

The tests were all too real. And sadly so were the mistakes.

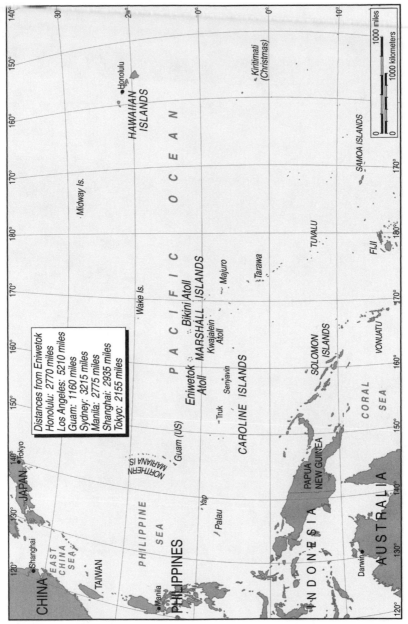

CHINA

Shanghai

Tokyo
JAPAN

TAIWAN

EAST
CHINA
SEA

Manila
PHILIPPINES

PHILIPPINE
SEA

Yap

Palau

NORTHERN MARIANA IS.

Guam (US)

Truk

CAROLINE ISLANDS

Senyavin

INDONESIA

PAPUA
NEW GUINEA

Darwin

AUSTRALIA

CORAL
SEA

SOLOMON
ISLANDS

VONUATU

Distances from Eniwetok
Honolulu: 2770 miles
Los Angeles: 5210 miles
Guam: 1160 miles
Sydney: 3215 miles
Manila: 2775 miles
Shanghai: 2935 miles
Tokyo: 2155 miles

Eniwetok
Atoll

Bikini Atoll

MARSHALL ISLANDS

Kwajalein
Atoll

Majuro

Tarawa

TUVALU

FIJI

Wake Is.

P A C I F I C   O C E A N

Midway Is.

Honolulu

HAWAIIAN
ISLANDS

Kiritimati
(Christmas)

SAMOA ISLANDS

1000 miles

1000 kilometers

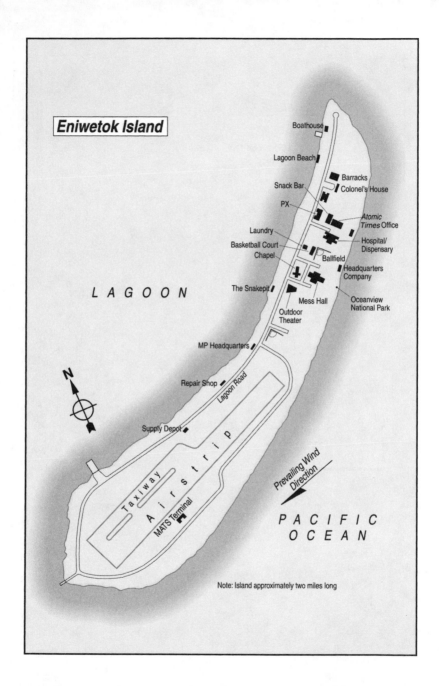

Eniwetok Island

Boathouse

Lagoon Beach

Barracks

Snack Bar

Colonel's House

PX

Atomic Times Office

Laundry

Basketball Court

Chapel

Hospital/
Dispensary

Ballfield

The Snakepit

Headquarters
Company

Mess Hall

Oceanview
National Park

Outdoor
Theater

MP Headquarters

LAGOON

Repair Shop

Lagoon Road

Supply Depot

Taxiway

Airstrip

MATS Terminal

N

Prevailing Wind
Direction

PACIFIC
OCEAN

Note: Island approximately two miles long

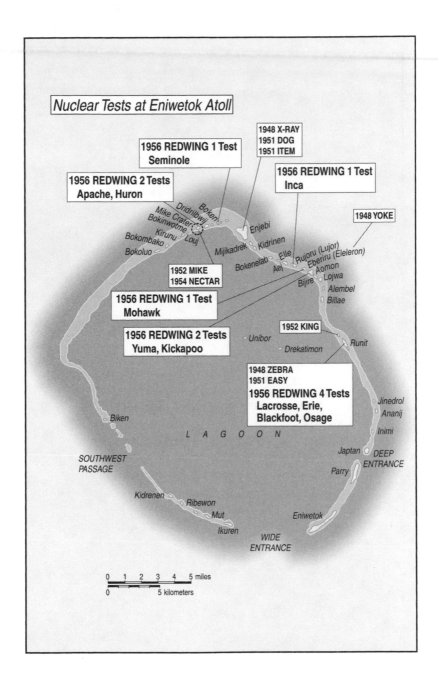

THE ATOMIC TIMES

PART ONE

Welcome to Eniwetok

WHITE MEAT!

"There's a woman behind every tree!"—that's what American soldiers were told in the 1950s before they left the States for Eniwetok.

Some men expected that exotic, erotic native women would provide them with the wild sex they had been looking forward to ever since adolescence. A few of them did not find out the truth until their plane landed and they looked out the window.

What they saw was a landscape stripped bare. After World War II the United States relocated all the local inhabitants to another island, and the army engineers leveled this one with bulldozers. They destroyed the foliage, cut down every plant, shrub and bush, and turned a lush tropical forest into a concrete slab.

One look around the airport made it obvious.

There were no trees.

The newcomers stared at a barren wasteland, and in August 1955, I was one of them. I had graduated from Brown University in June

1954, and that August the army drafted me for a twenty-four-month tour of duty. I was in the States during the first year and about to spend the second at the Atomic Energy Commission's Pacific Proving Ground in the Marshall Islands.

At twenty-two, I was younger and angrier than I realized and just as cynical. I had won first prize in the Worst Childhood Competition (I was the only judge) and had concluded before I became a teenager that everything was always worse than people said it was going to be. I had no reason to believe that would be any different in a place where the United States tested hydrogen bombs.

Fortunately, my misery years ended by college—I even volunteered then to hand back my Award. Finally I was happy, mainly because of my girlfriend Nancy. Partly because I had learned how to erase large chunks of the first fifteen years of my life. I had not yet discovered that suppressing memories was only a temporary solution and not an effective method of coming to terms with the past.

But in August 1955, it was the present I was coming to terms with—a year with Joint Task Force Seven, the official name of my new unit. Along with the other men on my plane, I was going to "provide support" for Operation Redwing, code name for the upcoming test series. The starting date was still classified—and not yet known to me.

I watched an MP corporal step aboard wearing a short-sleeved khaki shirt and khaki shorts, in striking contrast to our own standard, full-length uniforms.

"Welcome to Eniwetok," he said. "I hope you've had a pleasant trip. When I read your name off the manifest, answer 'Here' and leave the aircraft. There will be no talking. Gather to the right of the plane and follow me in single file to the briefing room. Don't talk to each other. Don't talk to the people outside. Don't walk under the wing of the plane. When you enter the briefing room, take a seat. Don't crowd the doorway."

He was short and thin and a bit prissy. Nothing imposing about his appearance, but we were all nervous—this was a new place and we didn't know what to expect.

He read our names off the manifest and obediently we answered "Here" and left the plane. I looked around and saw water, water everywhere—the South Pacific visible on three sides. This was a depressing flatland, and a sign provided us with that information in case we hadn't noticed: WELCOME TO ENIWETOK. ELEVATION 12 FEET.

There were a dozen of us, and once we were all on the ground, the corporal led his flock of numb sheep to the briefing room. On the way, we observed a bedraggled bunch of men of assorted shapes and sizes standing at the edge of the runway. The ones he had warned us not to talk to. They were deeply tanned and wearing khaki shorts like the MP, but the upper half of their wardrobe consisted of brightly colored, garishly patterned Hawaiian sport shirts. Which I assumed (correctly) was the off-duty uniform.

At first all they did was stare at us. I felt I was inside a zoo showcasing exotic species, though I wasn't sure if they were the animals or if we were. Then they shouted: "White meat! White meat! Some more white meat!"

Eniwetok's version of the Welcome Wagon.

The reception committee, of course, was not referring to our pale skin—and their preposterous attempt to frighten us almost made me laugh. But at least one member of our group took the implied threat seriously. Jason Underwood, a high school dropout from Mississippi, turned whiter. He was still recovering from his first glimpse out the window—he had actually expected to see the overgrown jungle that soldiers had described to him in the States. Now he stared at the ground and off into space, anywhere but at the men in aloha shirts.

That was a cue for the veterans, who now focused only on him. They rewarded Jason Underwood with his own personal rendition of "White meat!" I thought his knees were going to give way.

This time, three of the chanters broke away from their buddies and stood apart. I watched their faces slowly change: Their mouths curved down and their eyes—once playful—turned mean. They were no longer amusing themselves. They looked angry, and in a way I had never seen before. To my surprise, I thought they were hungry for crazy trouble, an unwholesome trio without rules, but at the same time I chastised myself for being too dramatic.

Then the ominous threesome delivered another encore of "White meat," and I observed a slight trickle of drool head southward to the chin of one. Dressed in vivid shirts and howling in unison, there was something unhuman about them. They were not individuals any-more—they had mutated into a single untamed creature of the wild.

As we entered the briefing room, Jason Underwood was visibly shaken and shaking. And even I was a bit unnerved.

The briefing room was small and bare. Plain wooden benches in the center of the room. Tables on both sides of the door, an MP standing at attention behind each one. Empty walls except for two photographs—of the army and air force commanding officers—and a sign printed in inch-high letters: THIS IS A SECURITY POST! ALL WORK BEING DONE ON THIS POST IS CLASSIFIED INFORMATION. WHAT YOU DO HERE, WHAT YOU SEE HERE, WHAT YOU HEAR HERE, WHEN YOU LEAVE HERE, LEAVE IT HERE.

A warning. The first of many.

The same tiny MP corporal waited at the front of the room and looked even smaller standing next to a gorilla-size captain—silent, rigid, unanimated. He would remain that way throughout the briefing, with only one apparent function—guarding the midget beside him.

The corporal began: "This is a security post! Let me tell you what that means. You are not allowed to talk about the type of construction going on here. The kind of work being done. The number of men sta-tioned here. The number of planes that arrive or leave in any given week. The names of important visitors or *if* there are important visi-tors. That information is classified and not to be discussed."

"Security post" was another way of saying H-bomb test site, and most of us already knew we would not be allowed to leave our new home for even a single day before our twelve months were over.

I had grown up on another island, Manhattan, but this one was much smaller, less than a square mile in size. Not a spot for claustro-phobes.

We all paid careful attention—the corporal was suddenly very much in charge. His voice was deeper, an intimidating baritone, and his brisk, no-shit manner ordered us to follow his rules. Or else.

"The following items are contraband and not permitted here without official authorization. Cameras. Drugs. Narcotics. Liquor. Sig-naling devices. Optical equipment. Film. Weapons of any kind. If you have any of these items in your possession, it would be wise of you to tell us before we examine your luggage."

The corporal zoomed in on one man at a time, stared for a few seconds, made his point, then shifted his eyes to someone else. Slow, deliberate, dramatic. Authority written all over his face. He had transformed himself: He was no longer small and, like a cartoon character, continued to grow larger and larger with every sentence.

"Because this place is isolated, that does not mean you can talk freely. While you are here, you will at no time discuss among yourselves the classified work you are doing. You will not discuss anything you see of an unusual nature such as new construction, unless you are doing so in an official capacity. You will at no time divulge classified information to any person on this island unless you are revealing it on a 'need to know' basis. Remember those words. 'Need to know.' If you hear a security discussion taking place among the men here, report this immediately to the provost marshal or the security officer. We cannot stress enough the importance of maintaining secrecy."

Isolated? It would have been hard to find a spot more remote, the very reason Eniwetok was chosen for H-bombs. So far away from the heavily populated areas of the world that it was considered ideal for nuclear experiments. We believed back then (incorrectly, as it turned out) that it would be impossible to damage the rest of the planet from there. Today we know better.

There was another reason Eniwetok was a popular choice for ground zero. The consensus was it would be easy to do without if anything went wrong. This was a place the world could afford to lose. A feeling, I would discover soon, shared by the military men who lived there.

"Mail censorship is self-imposed. Write home about the weather, about the movie you saw last night. Tell them what you ate for dinner. But don't say anything about the work going on at Eniwetok.

"You will be given a security examination to make certain you understand thoroughly what is expected of you. In order to remain on this post, you will have to answer all the questions correctly. No one leaves Eniwetok before he has been here twelve months, so you will be briefed and briefed again until you successfully pass the test.

"When I call off your name, you will step forward with your luggage and go to one of the MPs beside a table. He will examine your belongings to make certain there is no contraband in your possession. I tell you again, if you have brought any with you, I would suggest you tell the MP before he begins. After your belongings have been inspected, you will take your luggage with you and wait in front of the side door. Do not crowd the doorway. At that time you may again talk."

When the corporal finished, there was silence in the room. No sound except for names being called and White Meat scrambling to the tables for inspection.

When we went outside again, we were careful not to crowd the doorway. Finally we were allowed to speak.

Nobody did.

364 TO GO

We left the airport and "processed." First, we were required to take the security exam consisting of a true-or-false questionnaire.

"Classified information is only given out on 'a need to know' basis."
True or false.
"Eniwetok is not a security post."
True or false.
"A camera is a contraband item."
True or false.
Did everyone pass and move on to the medical exam?
True.

Inside the front door of the dispensary was a desk with a sign on top, REPORT HERE, and an arrow pointing to a clerk sitting in a chair reading an old newspaper. He asked his questions without looking up.

"Name?"
"Michael Harris."

"First name?"

"Michael."

He wrote down Michael Michaelharris. I didn't correct his mistake.

"Serial number?"

I told him.

"Age?"

"Twenty-two."

"Length of time here?"

"One day."

"If I had a year to go, I'd hang myself. Have a seat."

There were no seats.

The medical exam. Urine. Blood. Strip from the waist up for a stethoscope. A few knee jerks.

Everyone passed. True or false?

Next, new uniforms. Hundreds of unfolded khaki shorts and short-sleeved shirts in unmarked sizes were tossed haphazardly into large bins inside a musty room. The drill was to guess the right size and grab. Hold them up and keep them if they looked like they were going to fit. No one, including me, bothered to try them on.

Custom tailoring, Eniwetok style.

Our next destination: the chaplain's office. We walked through the door and watched him, seated in his chair with his head tilted back, holding a box of Chiclets above his open mouth and pouring them inside. When he had the desired number (I counted four), he sat upright and chewed while we stood around him in a semicircle. His jaw moved for a good ten seconds before he finally addressed us. "So what do you think about your new home?" he asked, looking at no one in particular.

The chaplain was in his late forties. Face tanned and leathery from the sun. Crew cut (white hair) so short he looked almost bald. He waited for an answer restlessly and, when he didn't get one, zeroed in on Jason Underwood. Still in shock from his first view of the island and the "White meat" crew.

Jason Underwood: lanky frame, large mole on his right cheek, long brown hair, blank eyes. His discomfort seemed to increase—if that was possible—when the chaplain singled him out. He shifted from one foot to the other and replied faintly, "It's okay, I guess. It's not very big."

The chaplain took a chewing break. He stuck his fingers above his tongue and between his teeth, removed the wad and parked it behind his right ear. He was ready to respond.

"The world is as big as your soul, young man," he replied in a deep booming voice particularly suitable for his profession. "The world can't be small if you're close to God. The smallness is inside *you*."

Jason Underwood blinked his eyes in confusion. "Yes, sir."

"What's your name?" the chaplain asked.

"Jason Underwood, sir."

"And what is your denomination?"

"Excuse me?"

"Your religion!"

"Protestant, sir."

"Protestant doesn't mean a thing to me," the chaplain answered with irritation. "Are you Baptist? Methodist? Episcopalian?"

"Episcopalian, sir."

"When was the last time you went to church?"

"A while ago."

"A while ago? What does that mean! A week? A month? Six months? A year?"

Jason Underwood's legs were shaking. "Er, uh, a year, sir."

"Aren't you aware of your responsibilities to God?"

"Yes, sir."

The chaplain took a card from a pile on top of his desk and handed it to him. "I want you to fill this out. And I expect you to be in church this Sunday. God gives you strength but He wants you to give Him something back."

"I understand, sir," Jason Underwood said, still blinking his eyes at a rapid rate.

Then the chaplain turned his attention to the rest of us. "There isn't a man in this room who can't use spiritual guidance, and it's important for every one of you to visit God's home every week. It's easy to get lazy Sunday mornings because it's the one day you can sleep late. But nothing good in life comes to us unless we make an effort. So let me get down to basics. We know the question: Who is the Savior? I want to hear the answer from you right now."

He waited but nobody said anything. Then he mouthed the words and used his hands like a cheerleader, encouraging us to shout them out.

"Sound off like you have a pair," he said.

And he got what he wanted, the words yelled in unison: "The Lord Our God Jesus Christ."

"Fuckin' A!" he said. "Now does anyone have anything to ask me?"

Jason Underwood raised his hand. "Sir, how do you spell Episcopalian?"

Laughter.

Berkowitz told him how it was spelled. He was an NYU graduate from Brooklyn with black, curly hair and a large hawk nose. We met on the plane, where I learned he was the world's most enthusiastic Brooklyn Dodgers fan. I rooted for their archrival, the New York Giants, and argued with him when he insisted the Dodgers were going to win the pennant that year and their first World Series ever in October. Unfortunately, his prediction ended up being accurate.

Berkowitz raised his hand. "I have a question," he said.

"Yes, young man," the chaplain answered. "What do you want to know?"

"It's about the Friday night services," Berkowitz said.

Outside the chaplain's office was a sign. CATHOLIC SERVICES SUNDAY 0830. PROTESTANT SERVICES SUNDAY 1100. JEWISH SERVICES FRIDAY 1900.

"Who is the rabbi that conducts the Friday night services?" Berkowitz asked.

The chaplain stuttered. He was standing now. *He* was the one shifting from one foot to the other.

"Well, actually . . ." he began while he searched uncomfortably for a way to explain the situation.

As Berkowitz had guessed, there *was* no rabbi on the island.

"Actually . . ." the chaplain repeated, "we expect to have a rabbi here before too long." He exhaled deeply, appearing relieved that this conversation was at an end. He thought.

"The sign mentions Friday night services," Berkowitz said. "Will you be conducting them yourself?"

The chaplain cleared his throat. "Well, actually, I'm a Methodist minister myself . . ."

Berkowitz had also guessed correctly that there were no Friday night services. The sign was there for show. To impress important visitors to the island. Especially important *Jewish* visitors.

The chaplain spent a few seconds awkwardly apologizing for the situation. Then he distributed his cards hastily. Then we left.

As we walked out the door, the chaplain moved the gum from his right ear back into his mouth.

Our final stop was the office of the island's security officer.

"Welcome to the Pacific Proving Ground," Major Maxwell said to us. "Welcome to Headquarters for the greatest force the world has ever known." He made a fist with his right hand and punched his left palm so hard that the noise of the impact was startling. "Believe you me, you're a lucky bunch of soldiers. You're going to see plenty of hydrogen bombs before you leave here. This will be the experience of your lifetime. I have one piece of advice for you. Enjoy it!"

The major punctuated his sentences with nods and chuckles. He had a squeaky voice, like chalk on slate, and his jaw moved up and down Charlie McCarthy–style. He never left his swivel chair during the indoctrination lecture and yet he was in constant motion: tapping a shoe on the floor one foot at a time, arranging and rearranging piles of papers, blowing away imaginary dust from on top, popping Sen-Sen into his mouth, taking notes. From a distance, he looked like he *should* have had bad breath, and up close that was confirmed, the reason no doubt for the Sen-Sen (which, in his case, didn't work).

"You're worried, you say, because H-bombs can kill people? Let me put you in the know right from the start. It ain't going to happen here. Day in and day out, we only think about one thing: your safety. On this island, it's safety first, second and third. The army and I are going to see to it personally that you're never in any danger. Oh, sure, there may be a little radiation now and then and from time to time, but no more than you get when you go to the dentist for X-rays. It's

going to be plenty better here, and we don't pull teeth in this place."
The major paused for a chuckle and then tapped the top of his desk
with a pencil as he continued talking. "You can take my word for it,"
he said, *tap, tap, tap,* "we're never going to bomb this island. And that's
not a threat, it's a promise!"

Berkowitz, who was standing right up front, laughed loudly.

The major looked wounded. "What's funny about that?" he asked.
Seriously and without irritation.

"Nothing, sir," Berkowitz replied, straight-faced now. "I just assumed you wouldn't bomb the island we're living on."

A grave expression took over the major's face, accompanied by
nodding. He replied without a touch of sarcasm: "I understand. And
I'm happy to inform you that you've assumed correctly. We'll never
bomb a place that treats us right. And you can take it from me, you're
about to begin a one-year paid vacation.

"A few men come here and tell themselves and their buddies this
is a hardship post. But they're not right-thinking men. You never had
it so good as you will out here. You only work until three o'clock. You
get good movies every night for just fifteen cents. You have good chow.
You wear comfortable uniforms. And you have a chance to save some
money. You never had it so good. A little isolation never hurt any man.
It's character building.

"And best of all, when you're off duty, there are a million ways to
have a good time. You can sun yourself, you can go swimming, you
can go boating, you can snorkel or play tennis or basketball or Ping-
Pong. There's no end to the list of activities we have here for your en-
joyment and pleasure. So I'm going to send you out into our little
world right now with a lot of good wishes and a bit of envy. I wish I
were lucky enough to be starting out my one-year tour of duty, but
I've already been here three weeks, so I've only got 344 days left. Any
questions?"

Berkowitz raised his hand: "If it's so much fun here, how come
you keep track of exactly how many days you have left?"

By now, Berkowitz had fully established himself as the class
clown.

The major harrumphed. "Soldiers, you're dismissed. We've all got
work to do."

.   .   .

We were finished processing but it was still early, and I knew immediately what *my* work was going to be. From the moment I had stepped off the plane and into the Eniwetok heat, I had been looking forward to a swim in the transparent turquoise water I had seen from the air. I made a quick stop at the PX to buy a bathing suit and changed in the barracks.

One of the veterans stopped me as I was walking out the door. "You have to wear sneakers," he told me. "There are stonefish on the bottom that change color with the background like chameleons. They have a poisonous sting that can be fatal within two minutes if anybody steps on one barefoot."

I was startled. "Nobody told us," I said.

"So what else is new!" He shrugged and I put on my sneakers.

I walked to the lagoon and, although I was wearing only a bathing suit, the sweat poured off me. The 90-degree-plus heat and 100 percent humidity made the prospect of swimming especially appealing.

The water itself was even more inviting and magical than it had appeared from the sky. In front of me was a placid, tropical blue pool, glassy smooth. Men were playing water basketball and diving from a raft anchored a hundred yards out.

The white sand under my feet felt soft and fine. I waded into the lagoon, and the clarity of the water made every detail visible. Schools of fish swam around me, and the sea world came alive with color: gold and pink and blue and yellow. I raised my arms and lowered my head, ready to dive in, when a single fish moved below me. Nothing unusual about the body and the tail. But the head! It had three eyes.

Mutated, I thought.

A victim of radiation?

And me? I asked myself.

I turned around and rushed toward the beach. Slightly dizzy and faint. What would happen to *me* if I spent more afternoons in the lagoon?

I decided then and there that I had absolutely no intention of finding out.

And I never went back.

LOCAL COLOR

ENIWETOK: TWO MILES LONG AND PEAR-SHAPED. THE LARGEST ISLAND IN ENIWE-
tok Atoll, a horseshoe-shaped coral reef of thirty small islands surrounding a sheltered lagoon forty miles across. The airstrip and 90
percent of the area were at the fat end, half a mile at its widest. The
barracks were at the thin end, a few hundred yards across.

The most jolting thing about Eniwetok was the absence of color.
All the buildings were silver—perforated aluminum. The concrete
was gray. The water, bluish green. The coral, white. And except for the
bottom of the lagoon, that exhausted the spectrum.

There was so much glare and reflection it was impossible not to
squint. Water and coral became a million mirrors that magnified a
dazzling sun and burned naked eyes. I was inside a pale hell made out
of white heat.

Even so, the island was drab without the reds and greens and
browns of foliage and earth. This was a barren spot surrounded by

ocean, a desolate concrete desert that deserved the name men gave it, the same as another security post—Alcatraz, the maximum-security prison.

Eniwetok and the famous San Francisco penal institution were alike in a number of ways. One of them was what the men living in both places called their home: The Rock.

The color was in the barracks—because of the occupants.

I was assigned to the Statler. At other army bases, living quarters were identified by letters. Here, they were named after famous hotels: the Plaza, the Waldorf, the Shamrock. Since the showers, toilets and urinals were located in a second building next door, these were luxury hotels with outhouses.

The barracks were long and narrow like the island. A corridor ran down the center, and rectangular cutouts in the metal on both sides served as doors to the rooms. Each one had an entrance in the middle, double-decker beds in the four corners (top bunk often unoccupied), and, next to them, footlockers. Wall lockers at the two ends, and opposite the door two dressers side by side plus a small table and chair.

I shared my room with seven other men, but it seemed like many more since everyone in the Statler congregated there.

Chester lay on his bed with a human skull on his chest, and the two resembled each other. Chester was so thin he looked like a skeleton with sandy hair and eyeglasses. He was a Korean War veteran, and the head resting on top of him was once attached to the body of a North Korean soldier he killed in battle. He cut it off and buried it in the earth for a week so insects would eat away the flesh and leave him with a clean souvenir. These days he held the skull tightly and stroked it over and over with the palm of his right hand, a man petting his cat, although *this* man no longer related to living creatures. Lost eyes informed everybody he had been through one difficult military experience too many, and the hunk of bone in his fingers was now his only friend.

Chester was silent—Mumbles talked continuously. But only to himself. Just as well since most of the time it was impossible to understand what he was saying. He had a small fishlike mouth that was always moving, although (like a ventriloquist) his lips never seemed to open despite his constant chatter. No one bothered to speak to him and no one referred to him by his real name. Which we didn't know anyway. Once I listened carefully (something I never saw anyone else do) and what I heard was: "The stars in the mirror are a shattered answer to anything made out of blood."

Kilmer—green eyes, acne, huge ears—contributed to the noise in another way. When he wasn't staring into space for hours at a time, he played imaginary instruments. Trombone. Accordion. Piano. Harmonica. Flute. Violin. He moved his hands and arms in the required fashion and made different kinds of humming noises—presumably the orchestra's music. Sometimes he abruptly abandoned his role as a one-man band and became the leader, waving an imaginary baton while spraying the room with his spit as he hummed.

Straletti actually had conversations. With Marilyn Monroe and Superman cutouts he had Scotch-taped to the ceiling. "Nobody in the world makes me horny the way you do," he said to Marilyn. "I wonder if you've got a platinum blond cunt to go with your platinum-blond hair."

An answer came back from Hawkins—red hair, close-set green eyes, and the inbred look of the backwoods mountains of West Virginia. He affected a high-pitched female voice: "Oh, Straletti, you make me so hot. And yes my snatch is real blond and it will get real wet if you just touch it once or twice."

His invitation over, Hawkins departed from the room and paced up and down the long hall corridor, shouting (in his normal baritone): "God, this place is boring. Why isn't there anything to do here?"

A different perspective from Major Maxwell's.

Eder took over for Hawkins, became the next Marilyn, and also spoke in a falsetto: "I'd love you to rub me where my hair is short, Straletti. Cause you've got the best-looking dick on The Rock and my pussy just aches for it."

Straletti, a roly-poly teddy bear with brown hair, smiled.

Muscle-bound Eder, bare-chested and bare-assed, moved to the floor for push-ups and sit-ups.

Straletti turned his attention to a comic book, one in a vast collection he kept in stacks on the floor, booby traps for men to trip over.

Hawkins returned and stared at Eder's muscular body: "Oh, Eder," he said in his normal voice. "You make me so hot!"

Eder smiled.

So did other men who looked over.

Not pint-size Craig, usually in constant motion but now quietly involved with his Victrola. He loved hillbilly music and put on his favorite, "That Do Make It Nice," with a vocal by Cousin Minnie Pearl. As always, he set the machine on automatic so it played this same record over and over. When the lyrics started, so did his hips. He twisted his body in rhythm to the beat and after a while he sat on the floor bobbing his head up and down as he read his Bible.

Wilson was also preoccupied. Today and every other day he focused only on his broom. Sweeping the floor around his bed for hours at a time. Cleaning up the same small area again and again. We all liked Wilson. Why? Because he didn't get in the way? Or make demands or bother anyone? Because he almost seemed content?

Freckle-faced Carl Duncan was (as usual) flipping through snapshots of his girlfriend Penny. Tousled blond hair, huge smile—to me, a Wisconsin version of Tom Sawyer. He didn't look like he had reached puberty, but Penny was one indication that he was past draft age.

Hawkins, still proclaiming his boredom, tried to grab the photographs: "I want to look at dirty pictures too."

Duncan held on tight and jammed them into his back pocket. Very private property. When he first got to The Rock (he told me), he didn't need snapshots of Penny. They were in his head. He used to think about her after Lights Out, and her features were so sharp and clear he could almost reach out and touch her in the dark. In those days it was hard for him not to say "I love you" out loud. Now he couldn't remember what she looked like without staring at the pictures for a long time, especially before he climbed into bed. A nightly refresher course.

Naked Eder continued to exercise. Counting sit-ups out loud. Very loud. And farting. Also very loud. Craig turned up the Victrola to drown him out. Immediately, men in other rooms turned up *their* phonographs to drown out Cousin Minnie.

Four Monopoly players shouted at each other. A man across the hall dictated a letter to his wife on tape. Loudly. There was also singing and whistling and men talking to their magazines and books.

Straletti, unable to concentrate on *Detective Comics*, told everyone to shut the hell up.

They didn't.

Then Hawkins yelled at Straletti: "God damn cocksucker!" He had just stumbled over the comic books on the floor. Or so he said. I happened to be watching and saw him *pretend* to trip. I assumed he was looking for an excuse to throw a punch. Which he did. A fist into Straletti's gut. With a mean expression on his face. Straletti hit back, at first almost playfully and then not so playfully. They also exchanged insults. Loudly.

Finally, I heard my favorite two words on The Rock: "Pipe down."

They came from Kevin Tonnello, the only man who could make the occupants of the barracks lower their volume.

Tony had been captain and quarterback of the football team at his small Southern California college, and now he was captain of the barracks. Usually he ignored the bedlam, but whenever the roar became too much for him, he made his feelings known, quietly and without apparent anger. The sound level instantly decreased.

Tony was a six-foot-two-inch golden boy, hair the color of sun, ocean-blue eyes and a low-key manner that commanded respect. The men called him Moviestar, a name that didn't flatter or annoy him and happened to be accurate. Sort of. He was handsome enough to make a living from his appearance, but unlike many pretty boy leading actors, his good looks didn't draw people closer but put them off. The softness in his voice rarely showed up in his features—a tough face that came with a warning: *Don't Mess With Me.* And no one did.

Unfortunately, he did not use his magical power to quiet the barracks often enough to suit me. Or Berkowitz, who lived in another room at the Statler. The racket in the asylum assaulted both of us from Day One. Berko carefully surveyed the inmates then: Chester and his human war trophy, Wilson's one-man sanitation department, Straletti talking to Marilyn, Mumbles talking to himself, Eder blowing naked farts, Kilmer blowing imaginary instruments, Hawkins restless and on the attack.

Early on, Berko turned to me and said: "I wonder what *we'll* be like in a few months."

Then he spotted a stunned, motionless Jason Underwood sitting in a chair. Face paler than before. Eyes frozen into an empty unblinking stare. Dead man with his lids open.

Quickly Berko corrected himself: "Maybe it doesn't take that long."

ALL THE NEWS THAT FITS,
WE PRINT

DURING MY FIRST WEEK ON THE ROCK, I IMAGINED THAT SOMEDAY PEOPLE WERE going to ask me: "What did you do when you were in the army?" And I would suck it up and spit out the truth: "I was editor of *The Atomic Times* during the H-bomb tests." I assumed that everyone would laugh at what sounded like a joke, and I would then explain that *The Atomic Times* was Eniwetok's daily newspaper.

The publication had a staff of three. At the top of the masthead was the name of the publisher, none other than the very same Major Maxwell, Security Officer, who welcomed me to the Pacific Proving Ground when I arrived.

The editor in chief was Franklin Ober, early twenties, snow-white hair, Boston University graduate, in his family's construction business outside Boston. He was the only divorced man I knew on The Rock, although actually his marriage had been annulled. On what grounds? The bride's and groom's immaturity, he told me.

I was number three, just plain editor and low man on the totem pole—an appropriate description of my status since the Operation was Redwing and every test in the series (I would find out later) was named after an American Indian tribe. For no sensible reason anyone was ever able to give me.

My second greeting from the major, like the first, took place in his office: "Welcome to *The Atomic Times*. The way I see it, this is the newspaper for the Headquarters of the greatest force the world has ever known."

The major was five-nine but the size of his body seemed to change constantly, even though he always stood, sat, walked and probably slept at attention. Unlike the small but assertive MP corporal in the briefing room, whose growth was produced by his manner and his ego, the major's continuously altering appearance resulted from changes in his mood.

During his larger moments, the major's chest and shoulders appeared to expand and his voice became louder and more intense. At those times, he wore bluster-colored eyes, and black bonfires blazed behind his retinas.

When he shrank, he looked like a suddenly punctured balloon slowly letting out air. He seemed to disappear inside himself, colorless and then invisible. The shouting interludes (which took place only when he was in his giant mode) seemed like an attempt to convince himself he was still there.

The major (no midget now) made a fist with his right hand, raised it high into the air and shook it hard. "You have a choice. You can get the best out of a situation or let the situation get the best of you. Use your noggin. It makes no sense not to use sense. It's only a matter of mind over matter."

He was facing me, but his eyes were focused somewhere behind my head. "We've got to work together out here. We're all peas in the same pod. We've got to be P-O-Z positive. Every one of us. Who does the army pick to be out here? You and me. Be proud they've shown so much confidence in us. You know how we can repay them?" He answered himself with the latest Gillette razor blade slogan: "Look sharp, feel sharp, be sharp!"

He continued to address the invisible audience in back of me, nodding vigorously, apparently in response to their applause. "Be proud you're American! An American soldier!" he yelled, making it sound like an order.

Then abruptly he stopped, looked at me with wide, wild eyes and waited for a reply.

"Yes, sir, proud to be American. Proud to be an American soldier," I repeated. My words seemed to bring him back to the here and now.

"We're proud too of the work we do here at *The Atomic Times*. I call it nuclear journalism." Chuckle. "I know you're going to fit in well. All you have to do is use your think tank and follow the rules. Number one, hard news is not allowed anywhere except on the front page."

"And why is that, sir?"

"Because no one is interested in news."

I couldn't figure out if that was a smart or a dumb comment.

"The rest of the paper is cartoons and sports, especially baseball and football scores. *That's* all anyone cares about. And we have one very strict policy: absolutely no headlines. Ever!"

I was about to speak when he interrupted me: "And don't ask me why. I don't like soldiers who ask me too many questions."

"Yes, sir."

"Is there anything else I was going to tell you?"

"I don't know, sir."

"I was talking to myself," he explained. With irritation.

Only later did I find out what he forgot. He had neglected to warn me about the Communists.

The Atomic Times was located inside the Information and Education Office, one more aluminum box. In addition to working on the newspaper, our duties included registering men for correspondence courses so they could earn high school diplomas. Now and then a few people signed up, but they dropped out quickly. The Rock was not a motivating place.

Ober and I spent most of our time putting out the paper and, mechanically at least, it was not easy. The mimeograph was an antique and functioned only because Ober was pretty good at using pliers and a screwdriver. My own contribution was to slam the machine hard with my fist. And to swear. Sometimes that worked better.

The Atomic Times was a single sheet folded in half to make a four-page paper. There was a drawing of a mushroom cloud on the mast-head and, in the top left-hand corner, a different "clever" phrase Ober and I thought up every day with a minimum of creative pride:

It's smart to be dumb. Don't talk about security.

Drive carefully. The life you save may be your replacement's.

The United Press teletype was our source of information. On days when important stories were breaking around the world, it was a struggle to cut down the articles to meet the major's space require-ment: No News Except On Page One. But his edict provided *The Atomic Times* with its motto (printed on top of the front page of every issue): "All the News That Fits, We Print."

We had a captive audience on the island since newspapers from the States arrived weeks late. But the only readers the major cared about worked in Room 217 at the Pentagon. Every afternoon we were required to mail them an envelope containing two copies of that day's edition of *The Atomic Times.* Who were they? Why were we ordered to send them every single issue we put out? How carefully did they look over what we printed? Those were questions the major obsessed over.

He wondered out loud how many of them were keeping track of us. Were they important? What about their rank? Were they generals? What did they like and dislike? What would get him reprimanded and what would bring him medals and commendations? There was never any feedback, so he had to guess what they approved of and what bothered them, and that tormented the major every day.

He decided that one way of staying on the good side of that Pen-tagon room number was to keep *The Atomic Times* at the forefront of the war against Communism. He was determined to be vigilant and never betray the trust of 217, and he did that by censoring every lib-eral statement he came across. He was terrified of what would happen to him if those mystery men (or women?) should find a reason to question his loyalty to his country.

His concern about America's potential enemies was always in-tense, but one story in particular pushed him close to the edge. He stormed into our city room one morning, picked up what turned out to be the offending article and read it. After he was finished, he held it by one edge as if it were a piece of used toilet paper and made a disap-proving face.

He glared at me, barely able to speak. "How dare you even consider printing this kind of shit in *The Atomic Times?*" he demanded to know.

Because it was the most important news story of the day. Though I had not yet figured out how to inform him of that fact.

"I don't understand, sir," I answered. And I *didn't.* Since I assumed he could see why it was newsworthy.

"You don't understand. You don't understand," the major replied. He liked to mimic people by repeating their phrases.

I remained rigid and baffled, waiting for my publisher to explain his concern.

"I'm not publishing a Commie rag here!" the major screamed, suddenly nine feet tall. "This is *The Atomic Times*! We're not going to let pinko propaganda slip past us and get into our paper. Otherwise, heads will roll."

I looked at Ober and he looked at me. We were both confused. I, for one, was unable to believe Major Maxwell had taken *this* many asshole lessons. And yet I wasn't going to be an angry combatant on this particular battlefield. Not if I intended to die of natural causes.

I responded calmly as I stared at the piece of paper he was pinching the corner of with two fingers and waving in front of my face. "What you're holding, sir," I explained slowly and clearly, "is a speech by President Eisenhower."

A blank look from the major.

"He's president of the United States," I added.

The major scowled. At this moment he disapproved of me more than the speech.

I glanced again at Ober, who wore a smirk. Which he did often. When Major Maxwell was not looking at him.

"I don't care what he's president of," the major shouted. "This is an army newspaper. Cut out the Commie parts."

So of course we cut.

HEADACHES

THE HEADACHES BEGAN SEVERAL WEEKS AFTER I GOT TO ENIWETOK. THE FIRST one was behind both eyes and mild. Gone the next morning but back in the afternoon and much, much worse. Not like anything I had ever experienced before.

Small pieces of pain scrambled through my skull and grew larger every minute. Chunks of tears were hiding in my head, ready to pour out and twist me into one long scream. I was afraid I was going to pass out and I left the office and collapsed on the ground. An hour later, I began to feel better. Back to work, and that evening I was fine.

I woke up the next morning and this time there was throbbing, too. Above, below and in back of the pupils. Small engines behind my retinas grinding my eyes into slivers and shreds. I told myself I was lucky I had never been through anything like this in the past. A pathetic way of trying to stay positive.

I went to the dispensary for a painkiller. The only place on The Rock to get aspirin—and always "by prescription." There was just one doctor on the island—Dr. Hasbrouck—and he had to initial all requests for medicine, including plain old Bayer. No problem. I asked. I got. And that made a big difference. The headache didn't go away but it let up and became bearable.

No pain at all the next day. I had forgotten how good that felt and I was grateful. I let myself believe these episodes were over.

But the next morning pain took over my entire face. I went to the dispensary and this time aspirin didn't help. Slices of fire scalded and melted capillaries inside my brain.

I wondered what was happening to me and I started asking around, a panhandler searching for information. Do you feel okay? Any headaches lately? Eyes bothering you? Any strange symptoms?

Nobody had any complaints other than the usual lack of pussy. Eyes? Same as always. Most of the men said it would be nice if something *were* wrong. It would be a good way to get off The Rock.

I thought about the deformed fish. Radiation in the water. Maybe on land, too. And maybe *that* was the reason for the headaches. On the other hand, nobody else was having them (and besides, I was the only one who wasn't swimming, as far as I knew). That made me assume contamination had nothing to do with it.

I had no idea what the problem was but I didn't see the doctor. I kept making excuses not to. He's not an ophthalmologist, I told myself, so why bother. Besides, the pain will probably go away soon. I came up with a dozen reasons to put off a medical exam, but I was deluding myself and refusing to admit the real reason.

It was this particular doctor. Dr. Hasbrouck.

I was determined to stay away from him.

THE STATLER:
DRAMATIS PERSONAE

THE CAST OF CHARACTERS HAD CHANGED BY THE TIME I'D BEEN ON THE ROCK A month—some new faces and a few departures. Gone were Kilmer and the invisible orchestra, Mumbles and the incoherent monologues, Chester and the souvenir skull. Their twelve months were over.

Berko once asked me: "Do you think they were that way when they got here or did the island do that to them?"

I responded with a big loud resounding shrug. But I suspected the answer was "Both." Some were fine when they arrived, others were damaged and got worse with time.

I pondered Berko's question as I observed the new arrivals.

Noonen had brown hair and yellow teeth and a floppy body. The top of him leaned forward—his chest and his back seemed stuffed with weights.

The first sentence out of his mouth: "They're poisoning the water here."

I pretended I didn't hear him. Not Straletti. "How do you know?" he asked.

"I can taste it," Noonen explained. To me, he resembled the Ray Bolger scarecrow in *The Wizard of Oz*—but with a hunted look.

"What you're tasting is saltpeter," Berko told him.

"Whatever I'm tasting, it isn't good." Pause. "I know what 'they' are like."

"What *are* they like?" Berko asked.

"People who poison the water," Noonen replied, stopping the conversation.

Alfred Richter, a self-described poet, also made sudden, unexpected pronouncements. "We're living on the other side of the moon," he told us one afternoon.

"Speak to Noonen about that," Berko advised. "He says the problem here is the water, and I understand there's no water on the moon."

Richter didn't reply and probably didn't hear. He wandered around in a private world, occasionally scribbling words in a pocket-size notebook except when he was ready to communicate. He was tall and well built and played in the daily pickup basketball game (along with Craig and Duncan). He was The Rock's best rebounder, except when he stopped the action to write down interesting phrases that had just popped into his head.

Richter was not planning a career as a poet. He intended to become an architect, a psychoanalyst or a drummer. "Like Frank Lloyd Wright, Sigmund Freud or Gene Krupa," he explained. "Poetry isn't a profession. It's a way of looking at life."

Billy Byrne was another newcomer no one could help but notice. Short (five-six) and fat (over two hundred pounds).

"How come the army let *you* in?" Hawkins wanted to know.

He was still pacing up and down the corridor, saying The Rock was boring and there was nothing to do. Still looking for fights. And day by day he was getting meaner.

Billy Byrne sulked. "I wanted to do what I can for my country."

"Which isn't much," Hawkins replied.

Billy Byrne grew up in Kansas farm country and was a very

young eighteen. He had never been away from his family before, and homesickness was carved into his face. And yet he tried hard to be agreeable and part of the group.

"I want to get laid," Eder said.

"I know what you mean," Billy Byrne responded.

"I think about broads every minute," Eder said.

"Me, too," Billy Byrne replied.

"I've never felt this horny," Eder went on (louder).

"Stop feeling sorry for yourself all the time," Tony ordered, his quiet voice firm, his irritation carefully concealed.

Everybody knew he was talking to Eder. Except Billy Byrne, whose face apologized.

Eder shut up. Which didn't stop him from delivering his favorite sentence at least once a day: "I wish I could get laid right now."

But never when Tony was around.

Carl Duncan was no longer staring at Penny's photographs before he climbed into bed. He told me that no matter how long he looked at her now, she was always blurry after Lights Out, even when he squinted his eyes hard to bring her into focus. The only women he could remember clearly in the dark were the ones he saw in that night's movie or in magazines he had just read. Maybe it would be different, he told me, if Penny weren't wearing loose-fitting clothes in all the snapshots—they concealed her body (contrary to what Hawkins imagined). "What I'd really like is pictures of her naked, but even if I got up the nerve to ask her, who would take them? And where could I hide them in the barracks so the other guys wouldn't find them?"

But some men were unchanged. Wilson was still sweeping. Jason Underwood remained comatose. Straletti continued to read comic books and talk to Marilyn. Craig played and played and played "That Do Make It Nice" on his Victrola.

Berko was never shy about expressing opinions on any subject, and he still blurted out everything that crossed his mind. At the top of his hate list were the security posters that lined the walls of the corridor. One was all print: DOES HE HAVE A NEED TO KNOW? Another showed a pair of eyes above the words: BE SECURITY CONSCIOUS.

"Big Brother is watching us," Berko announced loudly and covered up the eyes on the poster with Band-Aids. "How else are we going to get any privacy around here?"

He was especially offended by a third poster, a drawing of a woman he called Big Mammy, an African native with enormous disfigured lips. Below her face was a caption: IF YOU'RE NOT A UBANGI, DON'T BLAB.

"Have you ever seen anything more insulting to Negroes!" Berko said. "It's so insensitive."

Tony was fully aware that Berko was serious but that didn't keep him from laughing. "Nobody joins the army for sensitivity! And how many Ubangis do you think there are on this island? Go find them and apologize for all of us."

Berko knew that the absence of color on The Rock included the men. "The same number that were in the major leagues before the Dodgers and Jackie Robinson integrated baseball. But they're not that enlightened around here. No Negroes. Period. Only white meat!"

For Tony, the conversation was over. He rarely said more in the barracks, except when there was too much noise or the fighting turned vicious and he decided to play cop.

The rest of the time he was glued to the one chair in the room and reading: Thoreau, Plato, Melville. And sometimes observing.

That was Tony. Not much to say. Over and out. Catch me while you can. There but not there. Here now, gone tomorrow. The elusive Moviestar.

But with me he was talkative. When we were alone, he didn't know how to shut up, and that might have been one reason he intrigued me.

Though for all his chatter, it took me a long time to find out who he was.

JERK-OFF TIME

———— ⚛ ————

Tony was competent at almost everything he did.

He worked as a typist in Headquarters Company, but his skills extended beyond the keyboard. I never heard of a broken machine he couldn't repair, including all the typewriters in his office (even the ones that had been discarded), the busted recorder of the soldier who dictated letters to his wife and (regrettably) Craig's Victrola.

Tony never exaggerated his abilities to make himself seem more important, so I knew it was true when he told me he was an excellent driver and pilot too—he took flying lessons in college. He said his hand-eye coordination was near perfect, and he knew the exact place and angle to strike a tree with an ax to make it fall just where he wanted (certainly the least useful talent anyone could have on The Rock).

Tony inspired confidence. He was the man you'd choose to be in charge during a crisis—or so I thought during my early days on The Rock. But he was not as amiable as he sometimes seemed. The friendly, low-key exterior masked a disgust he felt about "the negativity" around him. He hated to hear complaining—not just from Eder but from anyone—and he told me so many times. "The men should just shape up and adjust. If you've got to be in the army for two years, this isn't a bad place to spend one of them."

"You sound like Major Maxwell," I said.

"Don't knock him. At least he's positive. And he takes his job seriously. He's a career officer who knows it's important to maintain discipline."

"Like making sure our shoes and belt buckles are always polished." A dig at Tony, the sharpest-looking soldier on the island—he spent hours at a time making certain that *his* sparkled.

"A soldier *should* look like a soldier," he replied.

"Yeah. Especially here in a South Pacific sauna."

"You have to have rules. You can't run an army any other way."

I didn't like rules, particularly Major Maxwell's. He stared at our socks whenever he walked into the I&E office and made certain they were rolled—like his. Nobody else on The Rock wore them that way. When I walked out the door at the end of the day, the first thing I did was *un*roll them.

"The guys around here don't know the meaning of self-control," Tony said, scowling. "I hate men who are always feeling sorry for themselves. And making sure we know how they feel."

I didn't like it much either, but I was a little more forgiving than Tony.

"It's just a matter of mind over matter," he added. Oddly, the same phrase Major Maxwell used when he gave me his *Atomic Times* indoctrination speech.

The scorn Tony felt for his fellow soldiers was never greater than it was at night. During Jerk-Off Time.

On other posts, taps marked the end of the day. For the men of Eniwetok, it was the beginning of the most important hour: taps (not from a live bugler but a scratchy record) followed by Lights Out followed by the only period of total silence on The Rock. The calm before the storm. The drought before the flood.

The quiet lasted for fifteen minutes and ended with the brief squeak of a spring. More silence, then many more squeaks, one after another in quick succession. Gradually, other beds joined in and became part of the local symphony, instruments in an orchestra rising slowly to a crescendo.

But there was no pride in the music here. The men were uncomfortable drawing attention to themselves, so everybody kept his jerk-off sounds to a minimum. Careful not to rustle the sheets or fold the blankets or breathe heavily or shift around on the mattress. Careful not to sigh or moan or groan at the crucial moment.

But it was impossible to silence the beds, so each performance had an irregular rhythm: start, stop, start again. Squeak, wait, movement—but slower the next time in an effort to keep the springs quiet.

New men began as the early players finished, and the number gradually increased, reaching a peak after twenty minutes. Most of them managed to be unobtrusive, and the noise from any single bed was barely audible. But during the course of forty minutes, every set of soft sounds was multiplied many times over and echoed up and down the length of the barracks, particularly the squeak of the springs. The result was a clatter like the clanking of chains. Heavy-duty noise that made the barracks during the day sound like a library.

Tony told me that the nightly racket made him realize the men were making life worse for themselves. He said it was much better to stop wanting what you can't have than to spend every day being hungry. That's what *he* did. He went cold turkey.

"I'm as horny as the next guy," he told me, "but I decided not to think about women and I didn't. After a while I lost all interest. Even when I test myself and concentrate on the hottest moments I've ever had, there's no life at all down there."

He said it proudly, which gave me a moment's pause.

"It's easy," he went on. "All it takes is willpower. I know from experience."

Something I could vouch for personally, since he slept in the bed above mine.

Tony told me he was "practical"—that was the reason he broke up with Tricia, a girl he was taking out before he left for The Rock. "We were not exactly an item, but I guess I was dating her more than anyone else. Since we weren't going to see or talk to each other for twelve months, it would have been stupid to keep the relationship going. No point in kidding ourselves."

"What was she like?" I said.

"Black hair, blue eyes, fair complexion, large breasts."

I waited for more but he had nothing to add. I wondered if he even knew the answer to the question I had asked.

He said that on their last date before he shipped out, he told her that if she was still around when he got back, maybe he'd look her up. She was shattered, he said. She wrote him a few times, even though he had told her not to, but he didn't answer. "What's the point?" he said to me. Finally she stopped writing.

I was a different kind of animal. I lived for the mail I got from my girlfriend Nancy, and I wrote letters to her every day. Tony had *his* way of dealing with the island. Nancy was mine.

And during Happy Hour, I was a mere mortal who joined the other noisemakers at the nightly party. For me, it was the best time of the day.

ADVICE FROM A
PRACTICAL FRIEND

I FINALLY ADMITTED TO MYSELF WHY I WASN'T GOING IN FOR A MEDICAL EXAM. True, the doctor was not an ophthalmologist, but the reason I didn't speak to him about my headaches was because he made me uncomfortable. And I wasn't sure why.

It was not his appearance. Late twenties, blond hair and straight, even features. Clean-cut and wholesome. "Cute" is what the women at Brown would have called him. The men would have said he was "Joe College." Pleasant face. Cheerleader type. Classic White Bread.

What bothered me about him? I went to the dispensary often for aspirin. Sometimes he passed me in the hall and smiled warmly. At other times he glared—a blank, chilling look. Now and then I would turn around and catch him staring at me. And when I did, he never said anything. Didn't blink. Didn't look away. Just kept on staring. Was it like or dislike? His expression gave me no clue about what was going on inside his head.

And then there was the aspirin problem. Sometimes I went to the dispensary and got them (in a paper cup, two at a time, never more). But sometimes the clerk refused to give them to me. No explanation. Just a turndown. Yes, we have no bananas. Since the doctor had to approve all medication, even lowly over-the-counter remedies, I assumed that now and then he instructed the clerk to deny my request. I had no idea why.

I asked around to find out what the men had heard about him. The answers ranged from Nothing to Not Much. Berko was the only one with anything interesting to report: "He loves to operate. Go to the dispensary with a stomachache and you'll end up with an appendectomy."

"What about headaches?" I asked.

"Nothing major. Just brain surgery."

I laughed. But a wisecrack was not what I needed. I wanted a serious conversation. But with whom?

Tony? Why not! He was serious, all right. In fact, he was never anything else. Besides, he was practical. He told me so himself. But even though my own definition of the word might have been different from his, he was in his own way sensible and logical. Which, at this particular moment, I wasn't.

It was crazy of me to put off seeing the doctor. And to torture myself with thoughts that maybe it *wasn't* my eyes but something much worse. I couldn't keep the headaches out of my head but at least I could keep my fears from lodging there. I needed to force myself not to think about brain tumors, much less the C word. A simple matter of self-control. Tony's specialty.

I grabbed him when he came back from our outhouse. Where he brushed his teeth a dozen times a day.

"There's something I'd like to talk to you about," I said.

All I wanted him to do was tell me to stop being a jerk and get a physical examination.

"Talk to me? Sure." He reached for a jar of instant coffee crystals, which he always kept close. And, as he did throughout the day, he used his fingers to layer about half a spoonful onto his tongue.

"There's something I want to talk to *you* about, too," Tony said. And went first. "I got a letter from my father."

Surprising news since his father never wrote. In fact, the two of them were not even on speaking terms, and that applied to Tony and the rest of his family. Except for his Aunt Irene.

"He's pissed because he found out I'm having the army deduct money from my paycheck every month and send it directly to Irene."

She was his father's youngest sister, ten years older than Tony and his favorite relative from early childhood. But after she had a daughter by a man she refused to name or marry, Tony's old man, the family spokesman, announced they were all "disgraced" and wouldn't have anything to do with her anymore. Tony treated his family the way they treated Irene—he disowned them.

"Now what did *you* want to talk about?" he said.

Before I could respond, he was back to his father again. "You know what he said after Irene's kid was born? 'At least she didn't have an abortion!' But he's not the one I really blame. It's the God damn Roman Catholic Church."

The Church had been a favorite target of his resentment since parochial school, when the nuns smacked his fingers with rulers every day.

"But my old man has plenty to answer for, too. If he had *his* way, Irene would starve. As usual, all he does is criticize me. I have no intention of answering his fucking letter."

Tony said he was happy to be free of his family. And yet he was not free enough to stop talking about them every time he found the chance. And whenever he did mention them, he came alive—his voice turned seductive and an electric current sizzled through his eyes. At these moments, he spoke more softly than usual, and I had to lean forward to hear him. And when I did, he changed into a hypnotist and magician and created the illusion he was interested only in me. Displaying a hint of the charm he seldom tapped. Exposing himself as an unused person with just a single outlet for most of his energy.

"How come you never talk about *your* family?" he said. Abruptly.

My family? My mother died suddenly when I was two, of a rare staph infection incurable even today. My stunned father buried himself in work and became the man who wasn't there. We lived in the same apartment but I rarely saw him—and when I did, he was crying.

I was brought up by the German baby nurse my mother hired when I was born. Addicted to codeine. Eventually psychotic.

I was surprised Tony even asked me about my family but not surprised he didn't wait for an answer. Which was just as well. He had as little interest in hearing about me as I did in speaking about my No Parent Childhood—privileged and deprived.

While Tony continued to talk about his old man, I made a decision. I was not going to see the doctor. Maybe the headaches would go away on their own.

THE LIFE OF AN ATOMIC NEWSPAPERMAN

"WE'VE GOT TO USE SOME IMAGINATION AROUND HERE," MAJOR MAXWELL IN-formed the staff of *The Atomic Times*. All two of us. "We need to dig down deep inside and come up with exciting new ideas."

Our group was assembled in the major's office, where he sat in his chair and stared at the ceiling, a usual source of his creativity when he was in an inspirational trance.

He squinted his eyes in concentration. "My own brain action has latched onto a big one. Get this: Citizenship and Morality."

Ober looked at me and rolled his eyes. I shrugged my shoulders.

"Sounds good to me," Ober said with a straight face. He was a world-class ass-kisser.

I sought distraction at the top of the major's desk. There his sta-pler, Scotch tape and pencils (sharpened four times daily) were neatly lined up with their edges exactly even, arranged in a straight line he drew with a ruler twice a day (morning and afternoon). This preoccupation extended to the motor pool, where he made certain all the vehicles were parked six inches apart, no more no less, with their bumpers aligned just as precisely.

The major raised his voice and brought me back to his mission of the moment. "You've probably figured out already what I have in mind. The two of you are Citizenship—our newspaper stands for all the fine American ideals that are so important to every one of us. The chaplain is Morality. *He's* concerned with our spiritual side. The trouble is, we're two parallel lines."

His eyes remained focused up. Not on the aluminum roof, I assumed, but even higher in his current quest for divine assistance. His hands emerged from behind his desk and for an instant I thought he was going to clasp them in prayer. But no. He held them in the air, one above the other, to illustrate his words. "From now on, your job is to make these parallel lines merge." And then he pressed his two palms together.

I moved my own eyes back to his desk, where two framed portraits faced each other. In the first, his family was seated in a formal pose (without the major). His wife, Constance, managed to smile and look angry at the same time. His mother, Andalune, seemed (not surprisingly) like an older version of Constance. In the center and foreground was Petrie, a stern father, holding up a Purple Heart.

The recipient of this honor occupied the second framed picture by himself. Major Maxwell's younger brother Chip, the family hero, twenty and smiling, killed in action during World War II.

The major cleared his throat and looked at *me.* He insisted on my full attention. "I want the chaplain to write a weekly column, and I've got the perfect name for it: The Chaplain's Corner."

Chuckling and nodding.

"Perfect," Ober said.

MM: "That man is Mr. Right and Wrong and there's plenty he can teach us about life."

"You're absolutely right. Good point, sir." From Guess Who. Yours truly remained silent.

MM: "Speak to him and put a pen in his hand. We need his wisdom on our payroll. Any questions?"

I was not going to fall for that one again.

.   .   .

Ober, the editor in chief, appointed the editor to execute this important assignment.

The chaplain, when approached, was, well, flattered. He beamed
and nodded and tilted back his head and loaded up on Chiclets, which
he chewed at a much faster clip than the first time I saw him.

"This is a big responsibility," he told me, "and I'm honored Major
Maxwell believes in me. I want to say right here and now and for the
record that he's an excellent man who goes to church every Sunday.
And it's not every day you can go to bat for an outstanding individual
who sees the important aspects of life in just the right way."

Out came the wad of gum, which he now stationed in the usual
parking place, behind his right ear.

"As a matter of fact, these articles are right up my alley. We're
talking about my life's work—making sure everyone's moral compass
is in good working order. I can already see the first column in front of
my eyes. I'm going to call it 'Alcohol: The Enemy of Man.' Is that excellent or is it excellent?"

I blinked and said, "Yes, sir." To both. Although I did have a few
doubts, which I declined to articulate. Maybe the enemy of man, but
not the enemy of soldiers on The Rock. Who were, after all, stranded
on an island with almost nothing to do except consume alcoholic
beverages.

The chaplain went ahead and produced his column, and the publisher called it "reflective" and "profound." MM was probably the only
man on The Rock who did not take it for granted that the article was
some kind of joke.

But his energetic endorsement ensured a second Chaplain's Corner, and I was once more delegated to meet with the author.

What do you do for an encore? You take on another vice of equal
concern to the inhabitants of the Pacific Proving Ground—swearing.
His title: "Sinning against God by Using His Name in Vain."

I nodded when I heard the idea and assured our writer that his
second essay would be received across the island with as much enthusiasm as the first.

After I read the completed article, I knew the chaplain had outdone himself. He gave two examples of phrases we should never use under any circumstances: "God almighty" and "God damn." He typed them right there on his copy paper!

Did I think the major was going to react violently? Fuckin' A! Was I going to stick my neck out and suggest changes? Fuckin' No!

MM saw these words and realized at once that the column would be read by the occupants of 217 and would then be passed around the Pentagon from room to room to serve as an example of decadent moral values in the South Pacific. But he was able to prevent this career-threatening scenario from taking place because he had the good fortune to detect the offensive language before the words hit print. His face turned deep red and his fingers took appropriate action. He ripped up the pages, scattered them around the office and then told us to clean up the place.

The chaplain was summoned to the I&E office for an editorial conference. The major informed him that he was absolutely shocked that a man of the cloth would even consider using garbage like that in a clean, wholesome newspaper like *The Atomic Times*.

The chaplain's face turned the color of his white crew cut. "That's the dumbest thing I ever heard," the chaplain replied. "I'm telling people what *not* to say."

"But you *said* it," the major answered. "It's disgusting. Your column belongs in just one place." He pointed to the scraps of his article that Ober and I had picked up from the floor and tossed into the wastepaper basket.

The discussion continued for a full ten minutes until the chaplain informed the major that he was crazy as a bedbug. He went to the front door and, right before he slammed it in the major's face, delivered his exit line: "You're a God damn fucking son of a bitch cocksucker."

After that, the major slept late on Sunday mornings.

I am sorry to say that I was 100 percent responsible for bringing the next bit of trouble down on my own head. I was stupid enough to make a creative suggestion. Despite the fact that Tony had informed me there were three secrets to a successful military career (not including polished shoes and buckles).

1. Never volunteer for anything.

2. Always keep your mouth shut.

3. If you do have to move your lips, don't ever let anything
   come out that even remotely resembles an idea.

The one I did produce seemed pretty good to all concerned at the time. I suggested that we print advance reviews of all the movies screened at the outdoor theater at sundown every night.

And for the world's most loyal audience, I might add. Each evening without fail it rained in the middle of reel two, but nobody ever walked out. The sky was clear when the men arrived, and yet they brought ponchos or raincoats with them. *Semper paratus.* They came prepared not for a drizzle but for the inevitable torrential downpour that lasted at least fifteen minutes, loud enough to drown out the sound track but not dampen anyone's enthusiasm. The men put on their rain gear (and still got drenched), but even though they couldn't hear a word, they remained in place and stared at a silent film.

My idea was to have a staff member of *The Atomic Times* (who regrettably turned out to be me) screen the picture ahead of time so a review could appear on the day of the performance. That way, men on The Rock would know in advance exactly what they were in for. Which they did anyway. Since all the movies were old and Grade B or worse.

I imagined that if I commented accurately on the quality of the films, Somebody Up There (in Room 217?), concerned about troop morale, would send us new and better motion pictures. How could I have been that naïve and that dumb?

Maybe I was spurred on by a conversation I had with Berko. "How are they fucking us?" he said to me one afternoon, paraphrasing Elizabeth Barrett Browning. "Let me count the ways." Ways that Joint Task Force Seven (JTF7) went out of its way to make our lives worse.

He started off by mentioning the makeshift tennis court at the airstrip, where men put up a net and played a few sets when planes weren't landing. "Did you know that JTF7 refused to buy a net for us?"

I didn't. "Then how did we get one?"

"A few guys chipped in and bought it themselves. They ordered it by mail from the States, with their own money, and had it shipped to The Rock."

Berkowitz was definitely the antidote to Major Maxwell.

"You know what books they have in the library?" he asked.

"Plenty of Nancy Drew mysteries," I said. I went inside once looking for something to read.

"Not to mention teenage romances," Berko added. "And textbooks on cattle diseases and soybean farming."

Next he brought up the mess hall. "Fresh food is *never* served there, and I mean never." As if he needed to remind me. Everything was canned or frozen or powdered, as in powdered eggs (our daily breakfast) and powdered milk. Doughnuts, the specialty of the house, gave new meaning to the word "grease" and were the perfect accompaniment to the watery coffee.

The boathouse: "One rowboat for the entire island!"

And then the movies. One by one, we reeled off the names of all the current films that soldiers at *un*isolated posts were now watching: *The Blackboard Jungle, East of Eden, Picnic, To Catch a Thief, Mister Roberts, The Seven Year Itch* (with Marilyn Monroe!).

As I stood facing Major Maxwell at the I&E office, I imagined my reviews would bring all those films to The Rock. Instead of the ones we *were* getting: *Gorilla at Large* starring Goliath the Gorilla. *The Big Combo* starring Cornel Wilde.

I should have known my fantasy bore zero connection to reality. That was not the way things worked in the military OR in the Department of Defense.

I should have remembered another comment of Berko's: "I'd even settle for good year-old movies. Like *The Caine Mutiny*. Though maybe Captain Queeg is a little too close to home."

Most of all, I should have known how the major would react when I wrote, in my first review, "There's nothing big about *The Big Combo.*"

He let me know how he felt in his usual subtle way. He shouted. "Sentences like this will keep people away from the movies."

Even thunderstorms couldn't do that. But I kept that observation to myself.

"And the Post Fund needs as many fifteen-cent admissions as we can get."

I couldn't understand why we had to pay anything. And I never knew what the Post Fund was, even though I was hearing about it all the time. But even I wasn't dumb enough to ask what it was or what it did.

"And you're destroying morale," he added. "We have to be CONstructive and not DEstructive around here."

The major had gone too far. I took my responsibilities as a reviewer seriously, and I was forced to speak out on behalf of all past and future members of my profession. "If anything, it's the quality of the movies that affects morale," I said.

"Have you ever seen even one soldier walk out of a film here?" he asked me.

I started to reply when he announced that he was not interested in my opinion. And added: "I don't see anything wrong with the movies we show here. And I don't think the Pentagon does either."

Again I started to speak. All I intended to say this time was "Yes, sir," but once more he interrupted. "From now on, every review you write is going to be a rave. That's a direct order!"

I fretted briefly about artistic integrity and went ahead and did as I was told.

PART TWO

The Cuckoo's Nest

BY APPOINTMENT ONLY

THE HEADACHES WERE WEARING ME DOWN, AND SO WAS THE HEAT. SOME MEN liked the climate, hot and humid during the day, slightly cooler and rainy at night. Not me.

I was raining too. Pouring liquid into the few clothes I wore, carrying around the weight of a shirt and shorts drenched by flooding—cotton transformed into steamy lead. Even my bones were sweating. And worse, the heavy suffocating air smothered me. I always felt I was gasping for oxygen, struggling to breathe.

I wondered if the weather was contributing to my headaches. Not likely, but by that time I was grasping for explanations.

I didn't like the spray much either. An invisible enemy I could feel and never see. Coming at me from the ocean *and* the lagoon, drowning my body with a thick and sticky layer of moist salt. An intruder traveling through clothes and coating every inch of my skin. A gummy covering that seemed to move along my surface, like tiny wet ants crawling up and down the edges of my flesh. I always felt grimy and dirty, and there was no place to get away. No spot on the island far enough from the salt water to escape.

Not even soap and freshwater helped. I scrubbed myself until I was red, but the moment I stepped out of the shower the stubborn film reappeared. Something gluey was always clinging to me, and I never got clean. Men who wore glasses (which didn't include me) had one more problem: They had to take off their frames every few minutes and wipe the fog from their lenses.

The Salty Wet (as some men called it) attacked everything on the island, not just people. Iron and steel corroded, and proof of that surrounded The Rock: Old ships and tanks and landing craft from World War II lay rusting offshore.

Even aluminum deteriorated rapidly. And the heat and the spray and the headaches made me feel that I was deteriorating rapidly, too.

I was rarely free from the throbbing inside my skull, and I couldn't postpone the inevitable any longer. Finally, I went to the dispensary, reconciled to an examination by the doctor.

The front door opened onto a long, narrow gray corridor. On each side was a bench long enough for a few men to sit (and was full during "processing"). The walls were bare (S.O.P. on The Rock except for the security posters).

There was an overpowering smell here all the time—not the usual disinfectant or medicinal odor but paint and varnish. Which should have sent a clear message to me.

Beyond the benches, a gray desk almost the width of the corridor faced the front door. Seated behind was the same clerk who took my frequent aspirin requests. He had curly red hair, a slender build and hugely muscular arms strangely out of proportion to the rest of his body. He stared at me today without recognition as if he had never seen me before, the way he always did. He asked me my name. Which I gave him. And which he wrote down in his daily logbook. I noticed my name appeared there more than anyone else's.

This morning, as on other days, his next question was always the same: "Why are you here?"

Until this morning my answer had never varied. "I have a headache," I would say. "I'd like some aspirin."

Today the request was different. "I'd like to see the doctor," I told the clerk. "My headaches are getting worse."

"Physicals are by appointment only," he said. "Do you have one?" He must have known that I didn't, since he was the only man who made them.

I shook my head.

"Is this an emergency?" he asked. "If it is, I may be able to fit you in this morning."

"I have another bad headache," I told him. "I get them frequently."

"No emergency there," he said. "I'll make an appointment for you for tomorrow."

I returned as scheduled.

"Name?" he asked.

I told him.

"Why are you here today?" he asked.

"For a physical."

"Do you have an appointment?"

"Yes."

"Been here before?" he asked.

I nodded.

"I didn't hear you," he said.

"Yes."

"Reason for requesting a physical?"

"Headaches," I replied, and he wrote down headaches in his log-book. Just as he had on every other day I was there.

"The doctor's busy but I'll squeeze you in," he told me. "Go to the examination room, last door on the left, and have a seat. Leave the door open."

On the way, I passed the doctor's office and saw him inside reading a newspaper, the *Atlanta Constitution*.

I sat in the one available chair in the examination room. The other, the doctor's, was behind his desk.

He entered a few minutes later and closed the door behind him. Instinctively, I stood. He gave me what seemed like a genuinely cheerful smile, warmer than any I had observed on the many previous occasions I had passed him in the hall.

"Let's see what we can do for you today," he said pleasantly. He spoke with a slight Southern drawl and, on the way to his desk, squeezed my right arm gently. Ordinarily, there would have been something comforting about that gesture.

Except . . .

Except on Eniwetok. There was a touching taboo. You never, ever put your arm around another man's shoulder (even when you were both dead falling-down drunk) or touched his back or arm or (God forbid!) sat on his bed. And if somebody walked down the hall toward you, you turned sideways so you wouldn't brush against him when he passed.

But not the doctor. Maybe it was different with officers.

He stood in front of his desk, picked up a folder with my name on it and opened it up. "Physical examination," he said.

"Yes," I replied.

He sat on the edge of his desk facing me and I remained standing. "Any symptoms beside the headaches?" he asked.

"No."

He nodded and seemed reassured. "Vomiting? Loss of balance? Dizziness?"

"No," I answered.

"That's a good sign," he said, smiling in a nice way. "Now take off your clothes." He walked over to me and stood just a few inches away.

I took off my shirt and sneakers and socks but kept on my shorts since I wasn't wearing underwear—no one did on Eniwetok. And it was my eyes he was going to look at.

"All your clothes," he said.

I took off my shorts and stood in front of him naked.

He moved close to me and shined a light into my left eye. "Open wide," he said.

Then my right eye. Again: "Open wide."

His left hand was touching the back of my head, and when he finished, he left it there. His right hand fell to his side.

"Just exactly where is this pain?" he asked.

"Usually behind my eyes," I told him, indicating the area with my finger.

His face was near mine, the way it was when he was staring into my pupils, and I could feel his breath on my cheek. I turned my head slightly to the side to give myself more space. And tried to back up too, but the examination table was right behind me against my legs, and there was no place to move.

"*When* do you get the headaches?" he asked. His left hand was at his side and the back of it brushed against my leg. Maybe it was accidental.

"No special time," I said. "Sometimes in the morning. Sometimes in the afternoon. There's no pattern I can make out. Sometimes I have the pain before I go to sleep and it's gone when I wake up. Sometimes it's worse in the morning."

"How long do the headaches last?" The back of his left hand rubbed against the side of my leg. Touching my skin lightly.

No accident.

"Anywhere from two hours to three days," I said.

And then the touch was not light anymore and I knew for sure what he wanted from me.

I almost said: "Keep your fucking hands off me."

And I almost laughed. I had worried for weeks about an unknown assailant inside my skull. When I finally faced my fears, I had to deal instead with another kind of assault. Gets your mind off the pain, all right.

And I almost slugged him.

But I stopped myself. This was a man I needed. The Keeper of the Aspirin.

I decided to be more subtle. Just let him know I wasn't interested— his cue to leave me alone and move on to some other individual who might welcome his attentions. I pushed his hand away.

"Lie down on the examination table. Faceup." No anger in his voice. Not even a sign of irritation.

I did as he instructed. Pleased that I had defused an uncomfortable situation.

"Do you ever see spots?" he asked, stepping back. He had gotten my message.

"No," I said.

"Do you see double?" he asked.

"No, never."

"Did you get headaches before you were in the army?" he asked.

"No," I replied. "Never. Not until Eniwetok."

And then his right hand moved. He began stroking my thigh.

Again I shoved away his hand. And this time I said something too: "I don't want you to do that." Keeping the anger out of my voice (the way Tony did). Still trying to be pleasant.

"You don't like sex?"

"Not with men," I answered.

"You don't have any choice around here," he pointed out.

"Yes, I do. I can choose to say no."

He shook his head. "That wouldn't be smart. I can make plenty of trouble for you if I don't like your attitude."

He smiled. All teeth. No longer clean-cut and wholesome—the cheerleader had left the room. In front of me, his face changed. Eyes narrowed. Fangs behind his lips turned razor sharp.

"On the other hand, I can help you in many ways. I have plenty of drugs in my pharmacy, and the right pills can get rid of all kinds of pain. Make the time pass faster too. I can also write a report about your serious eye condition. *That* could be your passport off The Rock."

I felt the largeness of his appetites filling up the room. Squeezing the oxygen from the air. Tugging at me and trying to pull me out of my own skin. Desiring only my outer layers, ready to dispose of everything else. Savoring the peel and discarding the orange.

"And all I have to do . . ." I began.

He finished my sentence. ". . . is be my friend. You and I could have a good time together."

A good time for you, maybe, but not for me.

And then he gave me a sample of what his idea of a good time was. He grabbed my cock in his fist and exercised his fingers.

"No," I shouted and pried away his hand. "I'm warning you. Don't do that." I turned over onto my stomach.

"You're warning me, are you? And if I don't choose to stop, what are you going to do about it?"

I didn't have many choices. "I'm asking you nicely. And if you don't listen to me, I'll report what happened here."

A big hearty laugh from Dr. Hasbrouck. "Now let *me* give *you* a warning. If you ever tell anyone I made a pass at you, I'm going to say *you* came on to *me*."

"And what makes you think they'll believe you and not me?"

More laughter. And his Southern accent became more pronounced. "Because I'm an officer! And we're the only ones who count around here. We make all the decisions, and no officer is going to take the word of an enlisted man over another officer. And one who happens to be a doctor too. In some places, doctors are gods. Here, I'm the only doctor, and that makes me more than a god. If *I* accuse *you*, *I'm* the one they'll believe, no matter what you say. That means I can touch you any way I want and there's nothing you can do about it."

He patted my ass and continued: "If I say you made a pass at me and swear to it on a stack of Bibles, you're dead meat, soldier. Do you have any idea what will happen to you?"

Then he told me.

Sam and Arthur. Found late at night by two MPs who sneaked up on them in the dark. Flashlights followed by an announcement: "The fun is over, you fucking faggots."

MPs with guns and billy clubs handcuffed the men (who had no weapons and no place to run to). Perps taken to the jail and placed on the floor of their cell in exactly the same position they were in when caught—naked except for sneakers, mouth of each man against the cock and balls of the other. The cuffs remained on their wrists and a rope was knotted around their arms and legs to keep them horizontal and facing each other.

An open house at the jail. Men invited to drop by and find out what fairies look like. Dozens RSVP'd in the affirmative and brought along their insults: "Fucking faggots!" "Sam and Arthur are fairy nice boys!"

Loaded rifles through the bars prodded their pricks and asses. At feeding time, buckets of breakfast slop were poured between their legs. Powdered eggs and powdered milk dribbled along their groins. "Go ahead and eat, but don't chew too hard." Laughter.

Visitors unbuttoned their flies and shoved their cocks through the bars and yelled some more: "I'll bet my dick turns you on, Arthur" and "I've got something for you to eat, Sam, and it's better than what they serve in the mess hall."

Then the spraying started. Prisoners drenched with piss until the stench got so bad an MP had to hose down the cell (and Sam and Arthur) with water under high pressure.

The doctor told me he was there and swore it was true. He said that after Sam and Arthur left The Rock, they were locked up in the States and not treated much better.

"Why are you telling me this?" I asked.

"I want to make sure you understand what will happen to you if you make me say you made a pass at me."

"I'm not going to tell anyone," I promised.

"And let's not forget the court-martial and the dishonorable discharge. They're not going to help you much when you apply for a civilian job."

"You don't have to worry about me. I'll keep my mouth shut."

His hands moved to my neck and my shoulders and he began massaging me. "There are many ways I can make you feel better. Think it over. And don't make your decision too quickly. All you have to do is make an effort."

I was searching for a response. "Yes" wasn't an option. But before I could find an appropriate answer (if there was one), he made the decision for me. At that instant, I felt his fingers prying into my ass. I jumped off the examination table and grabbed my clothes.

"You're in such a hurry," he said, smiling. And then he opened his desk drawer and removed a small container of aspirin. "One for the road," he said, offering it to me. "Just to show there are no hard feelings."

I extended my hand.

"On second thought," he said, withdrawing his, "I don't think this is the right time. Try me again tomorrow or the day after. Maybe I'll be in a different mood then."

I had no answer for him and for myself only questions. What was wrong with me? How could I find help?

WORST JOB ON THE ROCK

—⚛—

I KNEW SOMETHING WAS WRONG WHEN I WAS INSTRUCTED TO REPORT TO PERSONnel immediately.

I entered the office of a stocky dark-haired man in his mid-twenties. Bo Goldman, a Princeton graduate, would win an Academy Award twenty years later for his 1975 screenplay of *One Flew Over the Cuckoo's Nest*. In 1955 he was the personnel sergeant on Eniwetok.

I expected bad news, and he didn't disappoint me: "Major Maxwell and Doctor Hasbrouck talked to me about you. The doctor says you go on sick call every day and you claim to have headaches."

So far the complaint had nothing to do with sex. That was encouraging. I was quick to come to my own defense. "Not *every* day. And I don't *claim* to have headaches. I *do* have them. Blinding, painful headaches."

He continued: "The doctor says he's given you a thorough medical examination, and you're in excellent health. He says there's nothing wrong with your eyes or any other part of you. Except, as he puts it, your veracity. He insists you don't have headaches. He says you're making it up because you think that will get you off the island."

I disagreed quickly. "I'm not making anything up."

"The doctor says you're the only man on The Rock who has what he calls a headache problem."

I nodded. I knew all too well that was true.

Goldman: "The doctor says you're a liar. The major agrees and says you're a troublemaker. He says you're letting your country down. Both of them are outraged and they've ordered me to teach you a lesson. Make an example of you so no one else will ever be tempted to do the same thing. The major says the only way you're going to get off this island before your year is up is in a body bag."

I told Sergeant Goldman again that my headaches were real and persistent and very painful. I pointed out that a big problem was that aspirin was not available on The Rock without a prescription. *Aspirin,* for God's sake, which you can buy over the counter anywhere in the God damn United States, which happens to be a country I care about a great deal.

I went on nonstop until the sergeant interrupted me. "You don't have to convince *me,*" he said. "I'm only relaying to you what they told me. They're angry and upset and they've instructed me to transfer you from *The Atomic Times* to a new job. And not just any one. They want me to pick out the worst job on The Rock. One that involves hard physical labor and, if possible, keeps you out in the sun all day."

He waited for that to sink in. It did. They're talking about the gulag, I thought. They want me in an Eniwetok version of the Soviet Union's forced labor camps. Prisoners subjected to harsh living conditions. Isolation and extreme temperatures in both places, although the Soviet inmates worked in the other kind of severe weather—in northern Siberia.

"I can't give you a *good* job," Goldman said. "I've gotten my orders. I have to transfer you to a job that the doctor and Major Maxwell consider terrible. But I'm going to give you the very best job I can. You're going to spend your days cleaning up the Snakepit."

The Snakepit was where enlisted men on the island went to drink. Which they did plenty of, despite the chaplain's admonishments. Besides drinking beer and very hard liquor, they threw up—on the floor and the tables. They pissed in the urinals—sometimes. More often they pissed on the bathroom floor. If they made it that far. And from what I had observed of the hygienic habits of the consumers of alcohol at the Snakepit, they did not necessarily make it to the pot when they had to take a shit.

Right away I could see why the doctor and the major would consider this a terrible job. But it was better than the gulag, and I was grateful for the favor. I said thank you.

I never mentioned what happened in the doctor's examination room. What good would that have done? Besides, I suspected the doctor was making a preemptive strike. Sending me a message to keep my mouth shut or he would make life much worse for me in the future.

I left Bo Goldman's office and never saw him again. Soon after (days? weeks?), his twelve months were up and a plane flew him off the Cuckoo's Nest we were living on.

THE SNAKEPIT

———⚛———

THE SNAKEPIT (AKA DUFFY'S TAVERN) WAS NAMED, APPROPRIATELY, FOR THE 1948 Olivia de Havilland movie *The Snake Pit*—set in an insane asylum. *Duffy's Tavern*, a popular radio and television program, was "where the elite meet to eat." On The Rock, the Snakepit was where enlisted men went to feel sorry for themselves.

There were only two rules at the Snakepit. Number one: No officers or noncommissioned officers (like Bo Goldman) were allowed inside at any time—they had their own clubs. And number two: No liquor could be removed from the premises.

No enlisted men were removed from the premises either. No one was refused service, ever. A man too drunk to stand could get his nightcap handed to him in a chair or on the floor. If he had a friend around when he passed out, he'd be carried to his room. Otherwise he'd lie on the floor while soldiers stepped over him and around him (and occasionally on him), and he'd stagger back on his own when he woke up.

Sit down at your own risk. The chairs (as I remember all too well) were covered with vomit. Not always dry.

I swept, I dusted, I scrubbed. I wielded a very mean mop and became an expert at removing large quantities of human secretions I never knew existed. But it was the outside patio I preferred. At night it was quieter and a pleasanter place to be. And take it from one who knows, during the day it was a pleasanter place to clean.

My secret weapon was Duz, a popular laundry detergent of the 1950s with an omnipresent advertising slogan: "Duz Does Everything." On The Rock, the "everything" Duz did included cleaning the wings and bodies of planes contaminated by radiation.

Working at the Snakepit was not as bad as Doctor Hasbrouck and Major Maxwell had imagined. I spent the day by myself, and privacy was a luxury I had never expected on The Rock. I enjoyed this solitary existence—no hassle, no pressure. I played the jukebox for hours at a time, usually the same record over and over, like Craig. But no country music for me. I listened to a Cole Porter song that accurately described my feelings about my new job: "It's All Right with Me" (from *Can-Can*).

And yet my encounter with the doctor troubled me much more than I admitted. My morning in his office brought back memories I had buried for many years. The doctor was not the first person to touch me that way. He was the second.

When my mother was dying, she asked Fraulein—the German baby nurse she hired when I was born—to stay and never leave me. Fraulein promised she would, but taking care of me was not easy for her. She suffered from severe migraines, which she treated with large doses of codeine the local pharmacy gave her without a prescription. She was often drugged and slurred her words, though my father didn't seem to notice.

Fraulein was also addicted to me. She had three friends (a woman and a married couple) and no boyfriends. I was the most important person in her lonely life. She loved touching me. My chest, my arms, my legs, my *heine*, and most of all, my most private parts. Sometimes she fooled with me when I was sitting on the toilet. Always when I was in the tub. She scrubbed me with her fingers and soap and a washrag behind a locked bathroom door. Even after I stopped being a baby, my baby nurse continued to bathe me. When I was five and six, her hands lingered for a long while between my legs. The older I got, the more time they spent there. Mostly I managed not to think about it.

Besides, I didn't really understand what was going on. In those days, nobody referred to "child sexual abuse" in print or in conversation, so it was easy for me to pretend she wasn't doing what she was doing. I accepted a ritual that continued day after day.

I never considered telling anyone. And who would I tell, anyway? What would I say? If I did speak up, what would happen to me? I sensed I would lose Fraulein, the only "parent" I had, and then I would be completely alone.

I didn't even have friends. In those years, I was The Last Person Chosen. The boy who didn't fit in. The kid without a mother. The one they laughed at. The way they laughed at Fraulein. Who didn't wear makeup and had funny hair and spoke German.

When I sat down at an empty table in the school dining room at lunchtime, nobody else would join me. And if I pulled out the one empty chair at a full table, the entire group stood up and moved. So I brought a sandwich from home and ate by myself in an empty classroom.

The other students saw me as the kid who was different. And how could I have been anything else? My life at home was not like theirs, so naturally I was not like them. Or liked *by* them. I was weird, and in many more ways than they suspected (even apart from the sex with Fraulein).

My classmates got together on Saturdays and Sundays, but my weekends were like my school lunches. I spent them by myself. I sat in my bedroom and read *Wonder Woman* comic books. I had every issue ever printed because Wonder Woman was my mother, and someday she was going to return to Earth from a far-off planet and rescue me.

But at the age of fourteen, I rescued myself—I put an end to the bathroom years with Fraulein. For as far back as I could remember, I had paid a price for the luxury of having at least one parent, but the cost became too high when I reached adolescence.

Fraulein couldn't accept the change. Just as she couldn't understand that the bathroom touching was not acceptable. To her, I was just a child and that meant it was okay. So why did I have to grow up?

Why couldn't I be "her baby" forever—after all, she had been hired to be my baby nurse. She promised my mother she would never leave me, so why did I have to leave *her*?

Fraulein felt destroyed, and yet for one afternoon she turned into Wonder Woman (who I thought I didn't need anymore) and she came to my rescue. All during my childhood, she told me how terrible it was that my father rarely paid attention to me. Later that year—I was still fourteen—she told *him*. She was usually timid with my father, but this one time she found the courage to confront him. I wasn't there during the conversation, but I heard two identical versions afterward. My father, with deep regret, said he didn't realize how much he had neglected me, and he promised everything would be different in the future.

It was.

After that day, he and I had dinner together almost every evening and went to the movies on Friday afternoons. We talked and got to know each other, and I found out he was bright and nice and caring and generous. Only then did I understand how lonely and unhappy I had been during the years he wasn't there for me.

It had been almost a decade since I thought about the bathroom years with Fraulein, but the morning with the doctor changed that. I remembered.

I remembered moments I had suppressed when I was living through them. I didn't want to be inside the tub, and so I went somewhere else. In my head, I was at the movies or reading a comic book or walking down Fifth Avenue. I became a younger version of my father—I was the boy who wasn't there.

I knew (more or less) where and how and when Fraulein was feeling me, but I didn't allow myself to feel. And then, years later on The Rock, I was forced to confront emotions I never realized I had.

After I saw the doctor, I remembered too much—the excitement and the rage that were right there with me inside the tub along with the warm water and *her* warm hands.

After I remembered, I wanted to kill and didn't know who. I wanted to cry but I was too angry. I wanted to forget again and didn't know how. I had to start dealing with the past because I had no choice. There was one consolation: I could keep on reminding myself

I was not the same person I used to be during the first fourteen years of my life.

I never told anyone about the doctor's examination, and I never told anyone about Fraulein except for Berko (and only in a vague general way). He promised to keep his mouth shut, but he changed his mind on the afternoon some men in the barracks were bragging about how young they were the first time they got laid.

"Harris had sex when he was eight," Berko informed them. Older, in fact, than I actually was, but young enough to stop the conversation cold. Everyone looked at me in silence, impressed by a record they knew none of them could top.

"That's unbelievable," Eder finally said, so much envy on his face that it was clear he was a believer.

Other heads nodded in agreement but no one spoke. And yet the men continued to stare at me that afternoon with awe and respect. And after that day, I often heard them refer to my past in hushed and reverent tones.

It was a reputation I enjoyed having.

THE 1950s REBEL

———— ⚛ ————

FRAULEIN AND THE DOCTOR. I HAD "MY WORK" TO DISTRACT ME FROM BOTH OF them. I also had Nancy, the most important person in my life—on Eniwetok and for three years before. I wrote her every day and thought about her every minute.

We met at college, where we majored in each other. Nancy was at Radcliffe in Boston and I was in Providence, forty-five minutes away. We commuted back and forth on weekends, and sometimes during the week when we were desperate to be together.

We went to movies and plays but preferred to be alone, laughing and talking and never running out of things to say. We introduced each other to love and to passion and never learned how to keep our hands and our lips and our other body parts to ourselves. Week after week I was Gregory Peck taking the runaway princess Audrey Hepburn on a *Roman Holiday.* I was Burt Lancaster lying on the beach with Deborah Kerr in my arms while the waves rolled over us in *From Here to Eternity.*

But during the tame early fifties, it was not easy to live out those fantasies. The puritanical mood of the day was illustrated by the 1953 film *The Moon Is Blue*, banned by the Production Code and condemned by the Legion of Decency because the actors used words not permitted in a movie: "virgin" and "seduce" and "mistress"—even "pregnant."

The same standards prevailed at our colleges. Students were required to live on campus, but men were not allowed in the Radcliffe dorms or women in the rooms at Brown. I solved our problem by renting an apartment in Providence. I got three friends to share the cost and the four of us lived there in shifts. After I rented out the parking space, Nancy and I had a place of our own (sort of) for eight dollars a month. I followed the rules by keeping my room on campus, but I broke the rules too. Legally.

We had fun in our apartment but we also felt we were silently making a statement about the segregation of the sexes. In those days, there was nothing more important to protest—not even wars. Everyone seemed to feel that the Korean War (June 1950 to July 1953) and the Cold War with the Soviet Union were justified.

The mood of the campus and the country changed in June 1954, when another kind of school segregation was outlawed. *Racial* segregation. Students had plenty to protest then (beginning with the Montgomery, Alabama, bus boycott) but the Supreme Court decision came in the month I got my diploma—too late to affect my college life.

As an undergraduate, I showed my defiance in the limited ways available to me. I was a nonconformist at a university where just about everyone joined a fraternity, wore white bucks and went to the Saturday afternoon football games. Not me. Individuality was my mantra, down to my brand of cigarettes—mentholated Kools. And including architecture—I hated the new suburban communities like Levittown where each house was exactly like the next. Like James Dean, the most famous young rebel of those years, I was a *Rebel without a Cause*.

In my childhood, I was an outcast because I was different. I was lonely and wanted to belong and didn't know how. In time I learned, and at college I had many friends. No one seemed to mind anymore that I didn't fit the mold.

I was a 1950s rebel, but the *early* 1950s. Those were the boring years. Harry Belafonte, Mitch Miller and Liberace delivered mood music B.P.—Before Presley. Elvis didn't bring his excitement until 1956. Lucille Ball, Milton Berle and Jack Benny made us laugh, but comedy didn't find an edge until the last half of the decade with Nichols and May, Mort Sahl, Lenny Bruce. And the same with books: Jack Kerouac and the Beat Generation did not come along until 1957.

I was a member of the Beat-Up generation. Battered by society's demands that we never mention sex openly. There too I broke the rules. I wrote a poem, "Dog on Dog," that was published in the Brown Literary Magazine, about two dogs screwing on campus while students walked by and reacted silently.

The alumni did not walk by silently. They protested in record numbers by mail and by telephone and threatened to stop making contributions to the endowment funds.

I enjoyed the response. And if my ego was slightly bruised, it was pleasantly soothed at a one-room pad on Benefit Street.

The author of "Dog on Dog" wrote other kinds of poems on The Rock. I let Nancy know how much I missed her and needed her.

I got back letters filled with love. And much more.

There was a small bulge in each envelope Nancy sent me after I started work at the Snakepit. An important import that "customs" ignored many times a week.

"Mail censorship is self-imposed," the MP corporal told us when we arrived. That meant JTF7 did not examine the contents of my mail from Nancy.

The first time my special CARE package arrived, I ripped open the paper and immediately swallowed two of the many Bayer aspirin tablets inside. A slight headache vanished quickly.

In time, I built up a substantial store of over-the-counter painkillers. I had triumphed over the doctor!

Later I received another letter from Nancy (with the same slight bulge), but in addition to the small pills, she sent me some practical advice. She wrote what may have been the best letter I have ever received from anyone.

Nancy had discussed my headaches with her uncle, an eye doctor, and he pointed out to her that the tropical sun was bright and glary and even more so when it reflected off the water and the white coral. The blinding sun and its reflection could be causing the pain behind my eyes.

Nancy asked me if I wore sunglasses. If I didn't, she said, it was worth a try. Simple and obvious—though not obvious enough for me to figure out on my own.

Even though I couldn't buy aspirin on The Rock, they had plenty of sunglasses at the PX, and I found out quickly that they helped. That meant an end to the lowest period of my life on The Rock.

Before Redwing, that is.

Just when I was beginning to enjoy the days by myself, I had an unexpected visitor at the Snakepit, Capt. Bob Weiss, a friendly, energetic career officer in his late twenties, married, and also from New York. I had never met or seen or heard about him before, but we had a pleasant fifteen-minute conversation, mostly about everything we loved about our city. After he left, I had no idea why he had come.

I found out when he showed up again. The first visit was a job interview. The second, a job offer. Captain Weiss along with a major (who was *not* Maxwell) were in charge of the supply depot. The captain asked me to work there in what he called one of the most important jobs on the island. He wanted me to handle all the Top Secret requisitions for Operation Redwing. I had a Q clearance (one notch above Top Secret) so I was qualified from a security point of view. Apparently, Captain Weiss considered me suitable in the other ways.

I had kind of gotten to like the Snakepit, though not enough to say no to his offer. But before I accepted, I told him I would work at the supply depot on one condition. I wanted to be exempt from KP, unpleasant everywhere in the army, but on Eniwetok it was the gulag that MM and the doctor had envisioned for me. Sixteen hours of the hardest physical work and in a place where the hottest stoves outside of Hades elevated the already scorching island temperatures. I was not in a negotiating position, but I negotiated. And successfully.

I also had one important question to ask before my yes was official: "What does Doctor Hasbrouck have to say about this?"

"His opinion doesn't matter. He's not on the island anymore."

I was surprised. I knew his year would not be up for many months. "How come?"

"He was caught having sex with another man."

I was stunned. I thought he would be too careful to let that happen. I tried to conceal my reaction but doubt that I did.

"He was flown off the island quietly on the first plane out," Captain Weiss added.

Do not stop at Go. Do not go directly to Jail.

I had dozens of questions. Was he with an officer or an enlisted man? What was he doing when he was caught? *Where* was he? What happened to the other man? I started to ask but stopped after a few sentences. The captain refused to say any more. He wouldn't even tell me if the doctor's departure had anything to do with his job offer.

I wondered if Bob Weiss had figured out the real reason for my exile to Siberia after the doctor was unmasked. Maybe that convinced him (and other officers) that I was not guilty as charged of fabricating headaches to get off the island.

I sensed that he wanted me to tell him what happened during my "medical examination" but he didn't ask, and I wouldn't have told him if he had.

We never had another conversation about Doctor Hasbrouck, but he did say that afternoon that there would never again be just one doctor on The Rock. I was very pleased.

Eventually I came across one small clue about the identity of the second man. Jason Underwood mentioned that he had observed something odd. He saw an enlisted man being arrested for "homosexuality" and taken to the jail in handcuffs by two MPs.

"He was by himself," JU said. "I don't understand. How can you get into that kind of trouble when you're all alone?"

"We're living on a strange island," I replied.

Jason Underwood looked confused. I could see he was thinking very hard.

CAPTAIN WEISS AND
MAJOR VANISH

I TRANSFERRED FROM THE PUB TO THE HUB AND BEGAN MAKING REQUISITIONS for Operation Redwing.

The supply depot was a high rectangular shell of perforated aluminum (what else?) that dwarfed the men and the equipment underneath. The front entrance was in the center of one of the narrow sides and faced Lagoon Road, the only "street" on The Rock, running the entire length of the island next to the lagoon.

Inside, dozens of men were seated in an arrangement that overorganized Major Maxwell would never have tolerated. The desks, separated from one another by filing cabinets, faced four directions in no logical pattern.

In the rear were two officers, Captain Weiss and the major, at desks that faced each other in front of a back door only they used.

The weekday routine never varied. Up at 6:15, breakfast and then off to work. The supply depot was at the fat end of the island near the airstrip, and we took buses to get there. They left every fifteen minutes, and men lined up at the barracks bus stop like khaki-clad commuters, with one or two latecomers making a last-minute dash for the eight-fifteen.

At 9:30, a half-hour coffee break (standard across the island). Next to the depot was a shed without walls, and soldiers from the mess hall put out an urn of coffee on a table there, along with their infamous homemade doughnuts.

At noon, an hour for lunch, which included a round-trip bus ride to the mess hall. The workday ended at 3:00.

The depot major was large, had a potbelly, drooping eyelids and almost always looked like he was about to doze off. He never spoke to any of us and rarely to Captain Weiss. He never read a book or cleaned his fingernails or even examined the typed requisitions. He never smiled or laughed or frowned. He just sat and stared at the men and the walls with an empty look that occasionally shifted into Expression Number Two, an intense glare just short of anger that warned everyone: Don't slow down! Don't goof off!

We referred to him as Major Vanish because of his habit of rising from his chair suddenly, making a speedy exit out the rear door and heading for his jeep. Silently. No mean feat on that concreted terrain, since we could hear everyone else's footsteps. We assumed he walked on his toes because he wanted us to be unaware of his departure. When, in fact, it was his presence we were unaware of.

Next came the sound of the jeep's motor starting (a noise even he couldn't prevent), and we heard him drive off. Occasionally he made his entire journey on foot, and then his steps became loud again a few feet from the depot and softer and softer as he moved off into the distance. We never did find out where he went to. The Officers Club for a drink?

When our two superiors were both in residence, they maintained Order and Discipline. Talking was not allowed unless the conversation was with Captain Weiss (Major Vanish was deaf as well as mute). The only sounds were the clicks of typewriter keys and the rustle of paper as we took requisition requests from the In Baskets, inserted carbons into the forms, typed the necessary information, put the completed forms in the Out Basket and reached for another requisition request.

It was unusual for Captain Weiss to be absent at the same time as

Major Vanish. But when that happened, the mood at the depot underwent a transformation. The animals came out of their cages, ran around the office, hurled spitballs across the room, threw paper clips at one another, jumped on chairs and desks, told dirty jokes loudly and laughed at them loudly. Bedlam continued until someone detected the outside sounds of footsteps or a jeep. Then everyone abruptly hustled back to their desks, leaving no sign of what had just transpired except for the crumpled papers and paper clips on the floor.

The beginning of the lunch hour and the end of the working day produced a similar kind of frenzy. At those moments, sirens sounded across the island to let everyone know it was time to stop. Men in the depot leaped from their seats and ran for the front exit as if they had just been told that the first twelve soldiers out the door would be allowed to depart from the island immediately.

The rest of the time, we were an assembly line of clerks ordering supplies that ranged from furniture to pots and pans to automobile parts. Most of the men were on automatic pilot with no sense of what they were doing, lost in the monotony of mindless typing.

My own lot was somewhat better, though I have no desire to overstate my contributions. I handled the 143 classified requisitions for Operation Redwing, and mostly that involved filling in the blank spaces on the forms. I typed the name of each item I was requisitioning, the arms supply catalog number, the date of the order and the scheduled delivery date. These often included nuts, bolts and screws, commonplace pieces of hardware that had some special function in the tests. My requisitions were all Secret or Top Secret. Practically speaking, that translated as Destroy The Carbons. I also made sure each folder was stamped with the appropriate word, i.e., SECRET or TOP SECRET or just plain CLASSIFIED. Captain Weiss and I were the only ones allowed to handle these folders.

This was not a fulfilling way to spend the day but I don't wish to *understate* my contributions either. I was efficient. I made certain everything that was supposed to be ordered *was* ordered. That it was scheduled to arrive on time. That it *was* arriving on time. And I made sure there wasn't anything we were going to need that wasn't on order.

In addition, I was a good organizer and filer, and I named and indexed and cross-referenced all the folders so I could locate any one of them immediately. I was nothing more (or less) than a military secretary, but a good one.

That was how I finished out 1955. And it was late in the year that I learned Operation Redwing was going to start sometime after March 21. Did I find out from an announcement by the security officer, Major Maxwell? From an article in *The Atomic Times*? Of course not. The information appeared in another newspaper with a similar name.

On November 26, *The New York Times* printed an article on page four under the headline NEW REPORTS PUT H-BOMB TEST NEAR. The reporter (no byline) announced that "this country would make new tests of hydrogen and atomic bombs in the Pacific next spring," and although the Atomic Energy Commission declined to comment, "Congressional sources confirmed that a series of tests would be held."

Other men read similar stories in *their* hometown newspapers and they also found out about the spring start.

Up until this point, we almost believed the tests were a figment of someone's imagination. How could they be real when we had no idea when they would start? Now we knew, and although the date was not yet specific, at least men scheduled to depart after June 20 could be pretty sure they were going to be around for hydrogen bombs.

As *The New York Times* headline made clear, the tests were not going to take place sometime far off in the future—they were "*near.*"

The countdown had begun.

ATOMIC ATOLLS

WHILE I WAITED FOR THE START OF OPERATION REDWING, THE SIXTH NUCLEAR test series at Bikini and Eniwetok Atolls, I read through a bunch of newspaper clippings Nancy mailed me about the first five—Crossroads, Sandstone, Greenhouse, Ivy and Castle.

In 1946, Crossroads—consisting of two tests at Bikini Atoll, 140 miles from Eniwetok—studied the effects of nuclear weapons on 242 ships. One hundred fifty-six airplanes and 42,000 men were also involved.

Shot Baker was detonated ninety feet below the surface of the water. Shot Able was an air drop, and the bomb (normally referred to as "the device" by the scientists and the military) exploded at an altitude of 520 feet. And missed its target.

What did the navy discover (besides the need for better pilots and improved targeting)? Adm. William H. P. Blandy gave *Life* magazine a succinct answer: "It's a poison weapon."

The Marshall Islanders agreed. Many of them became sick from

Crossroads, but they had no word in their language for "radiation." After 1946, they used the English word "poison."

Comedian Bob Hope had another perspective on this Operation: "As soon as the war ended, we located the one spot on earth that hadn't been touched by the war and blew it to hell."

Operation Sandstone, in 1948 at Eniwetok Atoll, tested the "improved design" of atomic weapons in three blasts (X-Ray, Yoke and Zebra). They were all "tower shots"—detonated on fixed towers.

In 1949, the Soviet Union exploded its first atomic bomb, and President Truman, determined not to let the United States be overtaken in the nuclear arms race, declared publicly in January 1950 that it was his responsibility to defend our country against any possible aggressor. "Accordingly, I have directed the AEC to continue its work on all forms of atomic weapons, including the so-called hydrogen or *Super* bomb."

Operation Greenhouse, in 1951 at Eniwetok, consisted of four tower shots (Dog, Easy, George and Item), and two were "thermonuclear experiments," early steps toward the creation of a hydrogen bomb (or thermonuclear device).

America's first full-fledged hydrogen bomb was the initial test in Operation Ivy, November 1, 1952, at Eniwetok. "Mike," as it was called, was the largest bomb of any kind tested anywhere in the world up until that time—a nuclear fusion blast, with a substantial portion of the energy generated by the joining of atoms. Mike was more powerful than all the explosives used in World War II combined and produced a white fireball three miles wide. The mushroom cloud, sixty miles across after thirty minutes, climbed to a height of 120,000 feet.

What was once the island of Elugelab no longer existed. The land and the coral vaporized and in its place was a crater, more than a mile in diameter and 164 feet deep. It was filled with water darker than the rest of the lagoon, the same dark blue as deep ocean water.

Ivy was a two-test series, and the second device was dropped from a B-36H bomber fifteen days later at Eniwetok Atoll. "King" was the most powerful fission weapon ever detonated—its energy generated by the fission, or splitting, of plutonium atoms. But it seemed like an afterthought and an anticlimax because it was one-twentieth the size of its predecessor. King was misnamed since the title clearly belonged to Mike.

Mike was overshadowed by Operation Castle in 1954, a series that tested large-yield thermonuclear devices. And large they were—three of them bigger than Mike, providing an explosive American response to the Soviet Union's first H-bomb test in 1953.

Of the six shots in Castle, five (Romeo, Koon, Union, Yankee, Nectar) were hardly noticed. The first one got all the attention.

Bravo, on March 1, 1954, was by far the most powerful blast ever, though not intentionally. In the jargon used by scientists when a shot was larger than planned, Bravo "went big." This huge hydrogen bomb created the worst radiological disaster in United States history.

What went wrong? There were two problems, according to nuclear experts.

1. A scientific miscalculation resulted in the yield far exceeding expectations (involved was the "tritium bonus" provided by the lithium-7 isotope).

2. Unfavorable changes in the weather. The region's three basic wind systems (northeast trade, upper westerlies, Krakatoa easterlies) shifted before detonation—although there was plenty of time before zero hour to abort and postpone the test. That is, if Someone Up There in the military or the Atomic Energy Commission had chosen to make that decision.

But Bravo went off on schedule and exploded with a force equivalent to millions of tons of TNT, 600 to 700 times larger than the bombs that destroyed Hiroshima and Nagasaki. A mixture of radioactive materials, including pulverized coral, was forced high into the air, dispersed over a wide area by the winds and showered down on hundreds if not thousands of people, covering them with white, gritty, hale-like "snow." Otherwise known as fallout.

At least 236 Marshall Islanders, 23 Japanese fishermen and a minimum of 31 Americans were dangerously exposed. The victims inhaled "hot" ash, and radioactive particles whitened their hair, clung to their skin and caused radiation burns. They developed nausea, diarrhea, itching, eyes that smarted and watered and a significant decrease of white corpuscles in the blood.

The United States did not release information about the Americans, but the injuries to the Japanese and the Marshall Islanders were reported in detail by media around the globe. The reaction was worldwide outrage. The Atomic Energy Commission discovered that fallout presented a problem not only to human organs and skin and tissue. It was a public relations problem, too.

The AEC attempted to defuse the situation with calming statements and official apologies. Chairman Lewis Strauss wanted to "correct certain misapprehensions" after he returned from a trip to the Pacific Proving Ground. He reported that the exposed Marshall Islanders and Japanese were recovering rapidly (again no mention of Americans).

There was one problem with this announcement and those that followed in the next year. They were simply not true. Eighteen Marshallese children died (after playing in the "snow") and so did Aikichi Kuboyama, a Japanese fisherman aboard a boat with the unfortunate name of *Lucky Dragon*. At *least* one fisherman. Plus any unreported Americans. A minimum of nineteen dead. No rapid recovery from that condition.

On January 30, 1955, in an article in *The New York Times*, AEC sources were quoted again as stating that all the Marshall Islanders injured by radioactive dust had recovered and were "in excellent health."

On June 8, 1955, five navy doctors spoke to the American Medical Association at a meeting in Atlantic City. Their comments were printed in *The New York Times* under the headline: FALLOUT EFFECTS GONE IN 6 MONTHS. The doctors reported that all the Japanese fishermen were "improving satisfactorily" and all the Marshall Islanders had recovered. They also announced that "children appear to be slightly more sensitive to radiation" than adults. Was this their way of saying that eighteen Marshall Islands children had died?

Still later, another disturbing article appeared in *The New York*

Times—not so long before I arrived on The Rock. The paper reported there was still "lingering radioactivity in the water" of the Eniwetok lagoon.

Nancy assumed I'd want to find out as much as I could about the Pacific Proving Ground, but after I finished my research, I wondered if I would have been better off not knowing.

The AEC insisted that they understood what went wrong during Castle Bravo and were able to prevent any similar catastrophes in the future. But could I believe them—considering their credibility after *that* shot? Besides, these were the same people who were telling us it was safe to swim in the lagoon. And telling *The New York Times* something else.

Though I *was* reassured to learn there had been as few as two shots and no more than six in the five previous operations. If that also applied to Redwing, maybe I'd be exposed to less radiation than I feared.

Unfortunately, the opposite turned out to be true. I found out—after Redwing was well under way—that the number of explosions would far, far exceed any other test series and, in fact, equal all the previous operations combined.

Leave it to Major Maxwell to provide comic relief. We were assembled an hour after work to hear What Every Soldier Needs to Know about the Hydrogen Bomb. MM began his Atomic Lecture.

"A-T-O-M atom.

"A few helpful ABCs about the Big A.

"Let's take the horse by the tail, the bull by the nose and talk about the atom's incredible size.

"The atom may be compared to your solar system. Just as planets revolve around the sun, the electrons of atoms revolve in orbits around a central nucleus made up of protons and neutrons. Your proton is a positive particle, your electron a negative particle, and your neutron has no charge at all.

"The nuclear explosion is produced by chain reaction. At roughly a thousandth of a second after the explosion, a high-pressure wave develops and moves outward from the fireball. We cannot detect the nuclear radiation with our senses.

"Atoms can be split. By bombarding the nucleus and fast with smaller because break it up and nuclear fission a vast amount of energy releasing new neutrons bombarding and splitting a chain reac tion. A roentgen is the amount of radiation. That's how the bomb works. Classified. Don't write home."

The major looked up. The scripted gibberish was at an end, and he now addressed us casually. Soldier to soldier.

"As I've told you before, around here it's safety first, second and third. We're so concerned about each and every one of you that we've made certain every soldier, with absitively and posolutely no exceptions, will have his own pair of high-density goggles to wear during the explosions. That's important. I kid you not. Look at the fireball without your goggles and you can say toodle-loo to your eyes. I don't want to scare you, but you need to know we take that seriously. No one should be blind to these problems. [Chuckle.] We always have your interests at heart."

At this point, the major looked around. "Any questions?"

Did I just imagine he was praying for silence?

No such luck.

Richter, our resident poet, psychoanalyst and basketball player, held up the article from *The New York Times* announcing the start of the tests. It was yellow with age.

"Will Operation Redwing begin in the spring?" he asked. He had been drinking straight bourbon at the Snakepit from the time he left work and was now slurring his words. The major, of course, didn't notice.

MM sighed. "That's classified, soldier. Nobody can give you that information unless it's on a 'need to know' basis. As a matter of fact, I don't know the answer myself. Anyone else have a question?"

As a matter of fact, yes. Fat Billy Byrne, of all people, raised his hand. "What responsibilities will we have during the actual blasts?"

"Good question, soldier. Just the usual S.O.P. Stand tall and follow orders."

Noonen's turn: "Are you going to do anything about the water around here?"

MM: "I don't understand."

Noonen (mumbling): "That's okay. You wouldn't tell us anyway."

Berko was next: "What is the nucleus bombarded with to break it up into two smaller nuclei and release a vast amount of energy?"

Major Maxwell looked stunned and stood in front of us speechless. He searched through his prepared material, but the answer was not on the list the army had provided him to deal with expected questions.

The incredible shrinking major was so tiny now that I could not have found him with a microscope.

THE COLONEL'S FURNITURE

FOR ME, THE ONLY REASSURING PART OF MAJOR MAXWELL'S LECTURE INVOLVED the high-density goggles. He told us they were important, and I knew they had been ordered since I had typed the requisition myself. Later, I was asked to turn my original requisition into two, one for the officers and a second for the rest of us—the grunts.

But a few days after the atomic lecture, I found a note in my In Box from Captain Weiss telling me to requisition new furniture for the colonel's house. He provided me with details about the sofa, the chairs and the rest of the furniture along with specifics about the fabrics to be used for upholstery.

Underneath was a second note from the captain instructing me to put through a cancellation order for Requisition Number 76. Reason for cancellation? "Not essential." And what was Requisition 76 for? High-density goggles for the enlisted men.

I picked up these pieces of paper and held them the way Major Maxwell had once held President Eisenhower's speech: by the corners, as if they were used pieces of toilet paper. And I zoomed forward to Captain Weiss. "What *is* this?"

"A requisition," he said quietly. His innocent expression was supposed to inform me that he didn't know what I was talking about. But he knew.

"I don't understand what's going on here," I said, reaching for my own innocent expression. "Why do you want a furniture requisition stamped *Top Secret* and *Highest Priority?*"

"Because it's important," the captain told me.

I was now in interrogation mode. Very unseemly behavior considering our respective ranks. But I didn't care. What was he going to do? Send me back to the Snakepit? Besides, I had carefully arranged the files so that I could find anything and everything in ten seconds or less. And nobody else would be able to find anything. Ever.

"And it will get here faster if we classify it," the captain added.

Not to mention that no one without a clearance (i.e., most of the army Stateside) could find out what we were doing and make trouble for us. "Wouldn't I be breaking the rules if I gave household goods the highest shipping priority?" I maintained my innocent expression, though by now he had dropped his.

"Now I wouldn't put it that way," Captain Weiss said. "And I can vouch for the fact that the colonel's old furniture is *really* old."

To his credit, he smiled. And only allowed the edges of his mouth to curl up in that expression because he thought of me as a friend (and vice versa). He had said to me more than once that we should get together back in the States, although he never considered getting together after work on a one-mile-square island. Here, oil and water did not mix. As evidence: the two separate goggle requisitions.

"*Now* I understand!" I replied, tossing him one of my own smiles. Normally we discussed requisitions in writing only. I realized now it was to eliminate backtalk. From me, Private Mouth.

Captain Weiss let out a deep and heavy sigh. "I suppose you want to know why we're doing this," he said.

I nodded.

"Well, it's a simple matter of physics. There isn't room on the planes for us to fly in both the furniture *and* the goggles."

"I was never very good at physics, but just this week Major

Maxwell told us that we could damage our eyes permanently if we didn't wear goggles during the tests. Now, you don't think he would give us incorrect or inaccurate information, do you?"

"No, I don't." There was just a trace of a smirk on his face. I knew there was no possibility that *his* opinion of MM could be any different from my own.

The captain let out another sigh, this one deeper and heavier. "Look, I'm in the army just like you are. I do what I'm told to do."

I lasered back my response and not softly: "That's the Third Reich theme song!"

Captain Weiss was Jewish. My bullet hit him somewhere between his temple and his jaw. He *looked* like he was in pain, and he was. He lowered his head and stared at his desk. Neither of us said anything. I felt bad, but I didn't feel sorry.

Then the unheard-of took place. Major Vanish stirred. He looked over at us. He offered his services. "Maybe I can be of some help in this matter."

I doubt it.

But I did tell him about the atomic lecture. "Major Maxwell made a big point about the goggles—he said that if we didn't wear them, we'd all go blind."

"Goggles *are* important," Major Vanish said. "But the colonel's furniture is important too. Are you aware there will be many prominent visitors to this island during the tests?"

I wasn't, but it didn't surprise me to find out there would be a lot of them. "I sort of figured that," I said.

"Most of them will be eating and sleeping on ships," Major Vanish told me, "but now and then they'll ask to come ashore. And where do you think they'll go when they do?"

"To the colonel's house?"

"Exactly. Now, you wouldn't want any of our distinguished guests sitting on shabby chairs or leaning back on lumpy sofas, would you?"

I continued trying to persuade him. "I certainly understand what's important around here," I said. "But our eyes are important too. Major Maxwell told us that himself, and I know he wouldn't lie to us."

The major nodded: "I'm not saying that goggles aren't important, but we need to keep some perspective around here. You can damage your eyes if you're *facing* the blast without goggles. But all of us will be facing away and we'll even have our arms over our eyes. Goggles are helpful but they're not absolutely necessary. You get my point, don't you?"

Now it was my turn to nod. "Yes, sir, I understand. And while I'm at it, do you want me to cancel the requisition for the officers' goggles too?"

"Use your head, Private! Just how would it look to our important visitors if the officers didn't have goggles?"

"The same way it will look if they see the rest of us without goggles."

"Exactly!" Major Vanish said, looking pleased. "You understand my point. I'm glad you catch on so quickly. Now you shouldn't spend your time fretting about trivial matters like this. Go out and have a good time. Play basketball. Play tennis. Go for a swim."

"A swim?"

"Absolutely. You couldn't find a better way to forget about anything that's bothering you."

"Like wondering if my children will have three eyes?"

The major nodded enthusiastically. "Exactly. You get my drift. Now go out there and have a little fun! You deserve it!"

GETTING READY
FOR REDWING

THE ROCK WAS GETTING CROWDED—MORE AND MORE WHITE MEAT ARRIVING every day. The previously unoccupied upper bunks on the double-decker beds were now all filled. The jerk-off clanking was louder than ever and so was the mess hall (where the noise level almost equaled the barracks). The lines there were longer. The food was the same.

During the "off season" when I arrived, about 500 soldiers were stationed on the island, and yet you rarely bumped into anyone you knew. The Rock was like that—very few people but you seldom saw a familiar face. That didn't change as the tests drew nearer and the army population approached 1,200. Most of us stayed indoors, in the barracks or in our offices, so there were in fact not many faces outside to see.

There were more planes and they landed more often, sometimes seconds apart. They crashed through the sound barrier as they always did, producing the loudest noise most of us had ever heard. And they did *that* more often too. For the pilots, it was a game. They hit

Mach 1 every minute or so, shaking us up by shaking the flimsy aluminum structures down below. So that's what an earthquake feels like!

As the population and the activity increased, radiation badges were handed out. Small rectangular plastic discs three inches by an inch and a half that would allow us and the army to find out how much radiation we were exposed to.

But Major Maxwell said he didn't want us to get the wrong idea. Having badges did not mean we were going to be *exposed* to radiation. In fact, the opposite was true. They were a way of proving there was NO radiation on the island.

He said that after we left, the badges would be processed and the results would show there had never been anything to worry about. He told us that eventually we'd get the good news by mail.

Berko said he knew what the letter would say:

Dear Soldier:

We are happy to inform you that you are still alive.

Yours truly,
The Army.

The badge was on a key chain. But where do you put it? They didn't tell us and everybody wondered. Around your neck like a cross or a Star of David? Around your wrist like a bracelet?

Again Berko came up with the answer, and we followed his lead. "Over your prick, of course. You hook it around a belt loop and let it dangle over your cock."

But he never explained what to do at night after you took off your shorts. Loop it around a stiff dick? Beat your meat with a plastic disc for company?

For me, there was something sort of ominous about walking around all day wearing a disc that measured radiation, although obviously it was going to be important once the tests started. (It never even occurred to me then that many of the discs would turn out to be defective and that *all* of them measured only gamma particles and not alpha and beta particles—the ones we inhaled. So we would never know the true extent of our exposure.)

Many soldiers did not feel the way I did. I sensed some of them were saying to themselves: Look at me, I'm special—after all, how many men in the world get to watch H-bombs with plastic discs hanging over their pricks?

In my own cranky fashion, I preferred to define my individuality in other ways. Like smoking Kool cigarettes?

Operation Redwing was going to make history. For the first time ever, the United States would drop a hydrogen bomb from a plane. How did we find out? From our usual Stateside sources. I saw the details in my hometown newspaper, *The New York Times*, where the headline was on page two: H-BOMB TEST FIRST BY PLANE FOR U.S.

This was probably going to be the first time *anyone* dropped an H-bomb from a plane. Khrushchev claimed the Soviet Union had done it, but most individuals in a position to know were skeptical.

The "device" would be released from its bomb bay at an altitude of 55,000 feet and made to explode at 15,000 feet, the equivalent of a dozen Empire State Buildings and a height greater than the expected radius of the fireball—more than two miles long.

During Castle Bravo, the fireball touched the ground and sucked up tremendous quantities of earth into the radioactive cloud. The Atomic Energy Commission hoped to prevent a reoccurrence by detonating the new bomb at these extraordinary heights since the diameter of the fireball increased with the explosive force of the blast.

The test would be historic in another way, too. *The Times* reported: "It also will be the first hydrogen bomb to be tested in the presence of newspapermen and other representatives of news media." These men (no women present in those days?) had witnessed explosions of atomic bombs but never an H-bomb. Until now. Sixteen of them would be on the upper deck of the USS *Mount McKinley*, anchored off the Eniwetok lagoon.

If we were going to be fried by fallout, the press would be sautéed along with us.

The Times wrote about "a super super bomb . . . three times as powerful as the biggest hydrogen bomb ever tested." And in a later article said that this "improved model," developed by the Los Alamos scientific laboratory in New Mexico, was "expected to be more efficient than earlier models."

"Improved and more efficient." Might have been the slogan for a new consumer product, but I couldn't forget that I was one of the consumers they were targeting.

Journalists used the word "huge" to describe the weapon, but this monster bomb was going to dwarf all previous hydrogen fusion explosions and its luminosity would exceed five hundred suns.

Merely huge?

"There's something I don't understand," Jason Underwood said in the barracks one afternoon. "Why are we here? They're going to be exploding H-bombs. Why do they need hundreds and hundreds of soldiers on this island? Repairing cars. Preparing food. Driving buses. Putting out newspapers. I don't understand."

Berko responded: "The major doesn't understand either. Neither does the army. No one understands."

Jason Underwood looked confused. "Isn't it sort of pointless?" he said.

I decided to give him the same advice I often gave myself: "Don't think about it. You'll feel better."

Jason Underwood looked more confused.

By April there was a buzz on the island, and it was obvious in the barracks.

Straletti was not just reading comic books and talking to Marilyn but looking at newspaper and magazine clippings his family sent him in the mail.

"This is supposed to be the biggest H-bomb ever!" he announced with an excitement I had never seen from him before.

"It's going to be something to see!" Eder agreed.

He was the same good-natured fellow I had observed when I arrived, bright eyes and friendly smile. But now he supplemented his exercise routine with cards. He discovered poker, and the other players discovered Eder's money. He never won and never seemed to mind.

Nothing appeared to bother him except not getting laid. Which he informed us of daily.

"I can't wait for the tests to start," Eder said. He was counting push-ups out loud and was up to twenty-three.

"Be careful what you wish for," Richter told him.

Richter, the poet, was big on warnings, probably the result of his many sessions on the couch during high school. He lived in Manhattan, across Central Park from me, and he was one of the few people I knew in the 1950s who had been in psychoanalysis—and the only one my own age. He told us that his time on The Rock had helped him narrow down his future professional choices to just one—he was definitely going to be a psychoanalyst (and not an architect or a drummer).

As usual, Eder didn't know what Richter was talking about and continued doing push-ups. "Twenty-eight!" he yelled out.

"It's going to be better than the Fourth of July!" This from Bible-reading, Victrola-playing Craig, who had announced proudly on other days that he was a virgin and saving himself for his wife (whoever she was going to be).

"Are you saving yourself for the bomb?" Richter asked and laughed at his own joke. The only one who did.

The rest of us felt sorry for Craig—it was bad enough to be a virgin much less admit it freely. Although frequently the sympathy stopped. Some men liked to show him horny pictures and ask if he had a hard-on yet.

Richter liked to give Craig advice: "It's not healthy getting married without any sexual experience."

No answer.

More from Richter. "I notice you beat your meat every night. What do you think about when you're jerking off if you don't know what fucking feels like?"

"None of your God damn fucking business!" An unlikely response from Craig, a true disciple of the chaplain's—he never swore or took the name of the Lord in vain. For Richter, he made an exception.

"He thinks about your ass," Hawkins told Richter.

The West Virginian with the inbred look of the back mountains had stopped pacing and stopped saying he was bored. But he still tried to pick fights—with anyone except Tony. For him, Richter, star of the pickup basketball team, was an excellent candidate. Hawkins told Richter he had an athlete's body and a faggot's personality.

Richter had too much therapy to reply to that.

Hawkins's boredom had ended because Operation Redwing was beginning to make life interesting. Today he sided with the men looking forward to the H-bombs: "It's going to be exciting!"

"I know what you mean," Billy Byrne said.

Half a dozen others nodded. Including Jason Underwood.

Noonen remained in his private world. Which I became aware of when Berko asked him: "How's the water been tasting lately?"

Noonen: "I wouldn't know. I don't drink that shit anymore. I'm not taking any chances."

"Don't you get thirsty?"

"Of course not. I drink Coke." Available at the snack bar, where they sold soft drinks in rusty cans as well as cigarettes, nuts and candy bars. "I don't go to the mess hall these days. Those vegetables they give us? They boil them in their water. They're not going to get *me* sick. Coke and candy bars. I'm not eating anything else around here."

Berko: "How do you know they don't bring in special Coke made from their special water?"

Noonen stared at Berko suspiciously for several seconds. "You really think that's possible?"

Berko shrugged. "Who knows."

Noonen (nodding his head): "You're right. We all know what *they're* capable of." He sat on his bed, head in hand, and concentrated hard. He had plenty to worry about.

Carl Duncan was excited but he wasn't thinking about the tests—he had his own special reason.

"Penny's going to marry me!" he told me, holding up an envelope. He always went off to the lagoon after mail call to read her letters by himself, but on this day he hurried back to give me the good news. "She said yes," he shouted, even though I was standing right next to him. Normally he whispered, trying hard to keep his private life private. This afternoon he had no secrets. "She said she could never stop loving me, and we're going to have the wedding as soon as I get back to Wisconsin."

I was happy for him but surprised it had taken this long—Carl and Penny decided they belonged together when they were both four-teen. To me, they looked younger than that now and almost like twins: blond hair, round faces covered with freckles, huge smiles. I looked at the snapshots and I imagined them playing tag or hide-and-seek.

But on this day, his interest was in adult games. He asked me to help him pick out an engagement ring, and together we went to the PX, an island on an island, a place filled with high-quality low-priced merchandise from all over the world.

Walking through the door was entering an exotic international bazaar. Even the smell was different from anywhere else on The Rock—like just-opened packing crates—and the air was fresh and dry because dehumidifiers kept the merchandise from rusting.

This was a world of luxury, and sometimes I went there just to browse through the inventory: china, glassware, music boxes, sport-ing goods, silver buckles, sweaters, watches, leather belts, letter open-ers, cuff links, perfume, earrings, manicure sets, brooches, cosmetics, dresses.

Each time, I was transported back to civilization and I thought about places in New York I loved going to: Abercrombie & Fitch, where Hemingway and I bought sporting goods and clothes; the Majestic The-atre, where I saw the other *South Pacific*; my neighborhood Schrafft's for peanut butter, bacon, and jelly sandwiches; the Plaza Hotel for martinis or Gibsons.

Walking down these aisles on Eniwetok was a way of dealing with "Rock shock" on The Rock. But I had to be careful—too many memo-ries were dangerous. It was easy to get homesick, and there was no place to go to on the island to recover from that.

Today I focused only on the rock Carl was choosing for Penny's third finger. He and I parked ourselves at the jewelry counter and looked over all the possibilities. He decided on an engagement ring with just a single diamond, since the two of them, he said, were soon going to be just one. He chose the largest stone he could afford and handed over his hundred-dollar deposit.

Carl went back to the PX every day to admire his new purchase. We were not allowed to have cameras, but he got a photograph of the ring from a catalog at the PX and mailed it to Penny.

Carl's excitement continued, reinforced perhaps by the mood in the barracks—part ebullience, part impatience. Feelings that echoed the words that precede the start of the Olympics: "Let the games begin!" The men wanted something new and different to happen, anything to get rid of the oppressive boredom of daily island life.

But I was thinking about Castle Bravo. And wondering if one of these days they were going to have second thoughts.

SECOND THOUGHTS

———— ⚛ ————

ANY DAY NOW WE WERE GOING TO WATCH THE FIRST TEST. WE DIDN'T KNOW *which* day it would be, but maybe as soon as tomorrow.

The press was ready and waiting aboard the USS *Mount McKinley.* The lagoon was filled with ships, but they were too far away for us to read the names and see which one it was. But we knew it was out there somewhere.

Typewritten pages from the *Mount McKinley* were already traveling from the lagoon to Stateside newspapers and back to our island. A sort of boomerang of words. And for the moment, the power of that particular weapon seemed almost as intense as the one we were going to witness soon in the early hours of the morning. Maybe not mightier than the sword, but certainly attention-getting.

Two sentences made all of us take pause: "The most stupendous release of explosive energy unleashed on earth so far. And by far."

"Sounds very dangerous," Craig said and sighed. He had stopped playing in the pickup basketball game after work.

"No shit," Hawkins replied. "You just start to figure *that* out?"

Once Hawkins had paced and talked about how bored he was. Then he decided the tests would be exciting. Now the mood of the island was different and he found another way of dealing with life on The Rock.

He ran a razor blade along one of his legs and made a small gash above his right knee. Because he had a light touch, the cut was just on the surface but deep enough to draw blood. When the bleeding stopped, he found a second spot, held the blade carefully and made one more slice in his skin, this time on his left calf. Then he found another place and another, maybe nine or ten in all. He had discovered his own unique method of distracting himself from the tests. He spent hours at a time watching himself bleed.

No one seemed to notice. No one cared. No one commented. Except Richter. "That's a strange way to pass the time," he told Hawkins.

"*You* talk to *me* about strange," Hawkins replied, irritated that Richter had made him lose his concentration. "I'm expressing myself. Think of it as crimson poetry."

"You should express yourself to a shrink," Richter said.

Hawkins went back to the razor blade.

"Maybe we won't live through the test," Noonen said. The danger was not just from the water anymore. "If it goes off tomorrow morning, this could be our last day."

"What do you think, Moviestar?" Eder asked Tony.

"That's a dumb name to call anyone," Tony replied. The first time I had heard him bristle over his nickname. "It doesn't matter what a man looks like. It's what he's like inside that's important."

"Profound!" Richter said sarcastically. "Inner Beauty 101. The problem is you're ugly inside. On the outside you're a movie star."

Tony glared at him. Said nothing.

Craig: "Those small atomic bombs killed lots of people in Japan. This one is much bigger. I hate to think what could happen here."

Straletti: "We could be really fucked."

"I agree," Billy Byrne said.

Jason Underwood: "H-bombs kill people."

"That's true," Billy Byrne said.

Eder nodded and stared at the floor. Concern covered his face. He wanted someone (besides Major Maxwell) to tell him there was nothing to worry about. But reassurance was not forthcoming.

Jason Underwood found a bright side: "Wouldn't it be great if they blew up The Rock by mistake and had to send us home?"

"Asshole," Berko responded. "If they blew up The Rock by mistake, we'd all be dead."

"Maybe we'll get leukemia," Craig said.

Carl Duncan picked up on the disease angle: "I heard hydrogen bombs make you sterile." He turned his head away from us, but I could see the tears in his eyes. "Penny and I want to have a lot of kids."

And I silently expressed my own personal gratitude to the radiation badges. At that moment I imagined they would work. A nice shortcut, I told myself. I wouldn't have to wait and find out after ten thousand screws that all that sperm had no children inside.

Then a soldier I didn't know entered the barracks and muttered the two words everyone always wanted to hear: "Mail call."

The mail came every few days without a regular schedule. Mostly in the afternoon after work, but each time the arrival was unexpected. And each time we found out after someone learned the mail plane had landed, walked into the barracks and made a quiet announcement. Speaking softly and without excitement. Calmness that masked the frenzy he and everyone else felt inside.

This was the magic interruption, a surprise that turned noise into silence, movement into stillness. Two words that pushed down hard on the brakes and brought the barracks to a sudden, silent stop. For the moment, no more conversation about Operation Redwing. The afternoon had a new focus.

It took sixty minutes for the mail to be delivered from the airport and sorted. One hour until we had our letters from home.

Men went to their beds and stared at the ceiling, lit cigarettes and sucked in the smoke absently, looked at newspapers without seeing the print, played solitaire. The only noise in the barracks was the sound of Wilson sweeping.

Finally, the mail clerk repeated those same two words. But from *him*, no muttering. He yelled them out: "Mail call!"

The time had come.

MAIL CALL

THIS TIME THE TWO WORDS WERE ADRENALINE. SOLDIERS JUMPED FROM BEDS AND roared out of their rooms, a military charge complete with battle cries ("Here we go, men!") as we stampeded to the assembly area next to the barracks and formed a semicircle around the clerk who had mail in his hands and stacks more next to him on the ground.

I turned around and from where I was standing, I could see into the barracks. No one there but Wilson. Alone, the way he was years before in a Japanese prison camp during World War II. Living outside in a metal cage in the scorching heat for solitary months at a time. No fan of the midday sun then and now. And he was not going to like the artificial suns we were about to encounter. Maybe tomorrow.

Wilson preferred to stay indoors and maintain his pasty pallor. Today I watched him put down his broom and walk outside slowly. Move to the rim of the crowd a few feet from the rest of us and stand in the shade. Without saying a word. Nodding his head now and then in response to an imaginary greeting. A frozen face and empty stare directed at a spot just above the head of the shouting mail clerk.

The mail was not arranged alphabetically or in any other special order, but the letters for each man were together. The clerk yelled out names and the soldiers yelled "Here!" or "That's me!" as they rushed forward to claim what was theirs.

Straletti snatched two letters from the clerk, inspected them, smiled, opened them up and read them right away. He had twin sisters three years younger than he was, and their many friends were the only girls he had ever gone out with. These ex-dates wrote him often, and although their names usually sounded familiar, he could never connect them with faces, even when they wrote him about everything they had done together. Today's were from Gwen and Alice. Whoever they were.

Eder got no mail—he rarely did. He talked about his girlfriends all the time and how much sex he used to get, but he never received letters from any of them. Hawkins said that if they did exist, they were illiterate and didn't know how to write. But his women (fictional or real) were the subject of frequent teasing. Sometimes the men told Eder it was obvious he was a virgin too, like Craig. Often they ripped pictures of particularly ugly women out of magazines and taped them to the wall with the same handwritten caption: *Eder's girlfriend.* Eder never failed to laugh. But today nothing was amusing him. And that included getting no mail.

No mail for Wilson either. There never was. Each time he waited patiently, hoping perhaps this one time would be different.

Duncan had several envelopes and retreated to the temporary privacy of the lagoon.

I got a letter from my father and two from Nancy—with the usual bulges.

Tony was not as lucky. His Aunt Irene was about to graduate from nursing school and she was waiting to find out if she got the job she wanted most—at Mount Sinai, the local hospital. Tony was waiting too and expected to hear from her this afternoon. He didn't and his face displayed his disappointment.

Richter burrowed through the crowd yelling: "Make way! Make way!" He got one envelope and felt it carefully to make certain there wasn't a second underneath. Then he saw the wrong return address. "Shit, it's from my mother. Just what I need!"

A blond guy I didn't know stepped forward with his hand outstretched and screamed loud enough for everyone to hear: "I've got six letters from Janie!"

Billy Byrne reached for a thick stack and, as if it were accidental, spread the letters out fan-shape so everyone could see how many there were.

The clerk finished in fifteen minutes. He still had a few dozen letters for men who were sick or on KP. Or else, as he preferred to imply, they were his own.

Berko's mail included a package from his mother, which he opened at once. A box of cookies she had made herself. Berko hated his mother's baking and especially her cookies. He put them on the table and told us to eat as many as we wanted. Then he left the barracks.

Billy Byrne had seven letters and made sure everyone knew they were all from his girlfriend Margaret. He talked about her often and sometimes the men made fun of her.

"Does she milk cows with you, Billy Byrne?"

"Is she a better fuck than your pig, Billy Byrne?"

Billy Byrne didn't care what they said. He had a girlfriend and she wrote to him and in this world that was status.

Eder watched Billy Byrne begin reading the first of his seven letters. He had seen Margaret's picture once. Who'd ever believe a fat slob like Billy Byrne could get a girl that pretty?

"So what does your girlfriend have to say today?" he asked Billy Byrne.

Billy Byrne looked up from one of the letters. "How much she misses me."

"How much?" Eder asked.

Billy Byrne didn't answer.

"Read us the hot parts," Eder said.

Billy Byrne looked confused. He couldn't figure out if Eder was with him or against him.

"Come on, Billy Byrne," Hawkins said. "We all want to hear what Margaret has to say."

Billy Byrne's face brightened and (with a touch of arrogance) he said: "Sure."

He cleared his throat: "Dearest Billy Byrne."

"I like that 'Dearest,' " Eder said.

Encouraged, Billy Byrne continued: "I miss you so much. I think of you all the time."

"Get to the hot stuff," Eder said, and a few men who were not reading their own mail but listening to Billy Byrne's shouted out their agreement.

"I wish you were near me right now," Billy Byrne continued, a little hesitantly.

"And what would she do if you were?" Hawkins asked.

More reading: "I want to have your body against mine."

"I like that," Eder said. "And then what?"

Billy Byrne became more confident. He cleared his throat again: "I love kissing you. I love touching your weenie."

Eder: "Your weenie? She's kidding!"

Billy Byrne: "I feel good when your arms are around me. There's nobody in the world who gets me as wet as you do."

Eder: "Nobody in the world? How many other boyfriends does she have?"

"None, of course," Billy Byrne said. "She doesn't mean it that way."

Eder: "Doesn't mean it? That's what she wrote! Is she some kind of idiot?"

Billy Byrne was nervous now and tried to explain: "She loves me. She thinks about me all the time. That's what she said. It's right here."

I was watching. I had already finished reading the letter from my father (long and typewritten, dictated to his secretary Chiffy). I put the two from Nancy in my back pocket unopened as I always did. I had a ritual. I read them after dinner at the depot—I was the only one with a key to the office besides the captain and Major Vanish. There I would find out what she had to say and write her back in total privacy. Making it easier for me to imagine the two of us alone together.

Tony walked over to the table for a cookie but there weren't any. He turned the box over. Not even a crumb fell out. "Nothing left. What happened?"

"Billy Byrne finished them," Eder said.

Tony: "All of them? And he didn't leave any for the rest of us?" This did not improve his mood.

Tony walked over to Billy Byrne. "What's the matter with you?"

Billy Byrne shrugged.

"Let me see what you're reading," Tony said.

Billy Byrne folded up the letter, put it back in the envelope and held it close to his chest: "You can't look. It's private."

Eder: "Private? You're reading every word out loud."

"I want to see it," Tony said and reached for the envelope.

"You can't do that," Billy Byrne said. "The letter is mine." Petulant. Tears in his eyes.

In one swift gesture, Tony grabbed all the letters Billy Byrne had just received.

"You can't do that," Billy Byrne said again. The tears were no longer only in his eyes. They were sliding down his cheeks.

"He's already done it," Eder said, as Tony took the envelope Billy Byrne had opened, pulled out the stationery and read silently. When he was finished, he threw the pages and the unopened envelopes onto the floor, still saying nothing.

Billy Byrne tried to grab them. Eder got there first, scooped them up, and looked around the room with a triumphant grin. He began reading. Out loud. " 'Dear Son.' Dear Son? What is this, you're fucking your God damn mother?"

Billy Byrne sniffled. "Don't speak that way about my Mommadee!"

" 'Dear Son,' " Eder continued. " 'I hope you're eating three good meals a day the way you told me.' "

Eder looked at Billy Byrne. "Three meals? You eat six, you lying ton of lard. And every cookie you can get your hands on."

Eder examined the return address of every letter. They were all from his mother, and Margaret was not her first name.

"Your mother feels good when her body is next to yours?" Eder said. "She feels good when she touches your weenie? That's what you read us." He was laughing now. The other men were laughing too.

"You sick son of a bitch," Eder said to Billy Byrne. "You don't deserve any mail at all."

He waved the envelopes in front of Billy Byrne's face. "I'm going to rip everything into little pieces. *That's* what you deserve."

Billy Byrne panicked. "No, don't do that," he pleaded. "I haven't even read them yet." He reached out and tried to grab the letters but Eder held them beyond his grasp. "Don't do that to me," Billy Byrne begged. "I was just kidding! I didn't mean anything bad. Don't do anything to my letters. Please don't."

Eder sneered and slowly ripped them all to shreds. Billy Byrne was crying hard now: "Don't do that. Please don't."

"I've already done it," Eder said. And then he ripped all the pieces a second time and scattered them on the floor. Eder laughed again. "Here's your mail, Billy Byrne. Now you've gotten as many letters today as I did."

I had watched silently. Finally I spoke to Eder: "Why don't you leave Billy Byrne alone. Just because *you're* scared about the tests, you don't have to take it out on *him.*"

I sounded just like Richter. Though it was not intentional.

Eder, of course, had no idea what I was talking about: "You're crazy. I'm not scared about anything. You must be talking about yourself!" His expression told me to Mind My Own Business. "Anyway, I'm done."

And he was. I was trying to break up the party after it was all over.

I was irritated at Eder and at myself too. Why didn't I say something sooner?

No point in continuing the argument. Instead I looked for an apology from a second scapegoat. I turned to Tony and spoke quietly so no one else could hear. "Why did you egg Eder on?"

"Billy Byrne asked for it," he said.

"He's only a kid," I responded. "He was just trying to impress us. He doesn't know any better."

"Well, he'll know better now. We're helping him grow up," Tony replied.

That was Tony. All heart.

I didn't know *what* we were doing. But I could see what Billy Byrne was doing. He was on the floor now. On his hands and knees crawling along the concrete. Crying harder than ever. Picking up the scraps of paper that had once been his mail.

While Wilson continued to sweep.

PART THREE

Mushroom Clouds

Cover of the guide to Eniwetok presented to VIP visitors

THE FIRST TEST

S<small>ATURDAY</small>, M<small>AY</small> 5, 1956. W<small>E WERE AWAKENED AT</small> 4:00 A.M., <small>AND THAT</small> alone told us that today was going to be different from all the others. Then came the orders: *Be dressed and in formation outside the barracks at 5:00 A.M.* No other explanation given. None necessary. We were going to witness the first explosion in Operation Redwing. Code name: Lacrosse.

Tony checked his radiation badge to make sure it was tightly secured to his belt loop. We noticed and followed his lead.

When we left the barracks, Noonen said: "This could be our last day." Calmly and softly and without panic.

"I hope not," Eder replied.

Jason Underwood and Billy Byrne stared at the ground. Saying nothing.

Craig crossed himself. So did Straletti.

5:00 A.M. The company was in formation, and we marched in

single file to the lagoon. "Eyes straight ahead. Arms at your side. Stand tall."

We arrived at our destination: near the beach and facing the lagoon with our backs to the center of the island. Major Maxwell underlined that this was very important. The explosion had to be behind us. We must not look. If we face the blast, our eyes could be permanently damaged—even if they were closed. The major said we'd be told when it was safe to turn around and open our eyes.

And speaking of eyes, there were no high-density goggles for the enlisted men. No surprise, of course. As expected, all the officers had goggles. If they were unable to have children, at least they would be unfathers who could see.

6:10 A.M. The countdown. A voice came out of loudspeakers set up along the water. A disembodied voice. And we got the word: "H minus fifteen minutes."

Nobody knew who the voice belonged to and nobody cared (though a woman would have been a nice surprise!). All that mattered was—could he count minutes from fifteen to one backward? And he could.

Everyone stood at attention facing the lagoon.

Major Maxwell chose this moment for an inspection. We straightened out our khakis and stood erect. Wondering if there would still be erections later.

Armed with a flashlight, MM walked along row after row of soldiers to make certain we were all spit and polish. He directed his beam of light on our attire and explained: "We have to look our best for the Important Visitors."

By now, I knew all too well what he was thinking. The reporters on board the USS *Mount McKinley* might stare at us in the dark through their binoculars and write about our very unmilitary appearance. Or worse: photograph us! Around the world, front-page articles about this test would be accompanied by pictures of soldiers with unshiny shoes and tarnished belt buckles.

This group fell short of his high standards but, regrettably, there was not enough time to send the offending men back to their rooms to shape up. He could only hope the photographers would forget to load their cameras with film.

. . .

"H minus ten minutes."

We got a break. Attention! no longer required. Our standing orders: "At ease. Relax."

Nervous talking. Quiet conversations. Forced laughter. Throat-clearing. I was standing next to Eder. That was just how it happened to turn out. We were not having a quiet conversation. No nervous talking either. Just silence.

"H minus seven minutes."

I looked over at the water tower, in front of me and to the right, and I saw it was tied down with steel cables this morning. A structure at risk. We had been told the men were not at risk. No need to tie *us* down today with steel cables.

"H minus five minutes."

"Attention!" No more standing at ease. No more throat-clearing. No more talking. "You all know what attention means!"

Static over the loudspeaker. Was the disembodied voice getting nervous? The man next to me was. Our arms were not touching but I could feel Eder shake.

"H minus three minutes."

No one was talking.

Eder was still shaking. Mumbling too: *The Lord is my shepherd, I shall not want. He maketh me to lie down in green pastures: he leadeth me beside the still waters.* "Men wearing high-density goggles may turn around at zero hour plus ten seconds." *He restoreth my soul.* "Everyone else will wait thirty seconds."

No talking allowed but no one can hear Eder except me. *He leadeth me in the paths of righteousness.* "No one will turn around until an announcement is made over the PA system. No one, repeat no one, will look directly at the fireball at zero hour."

The disembodied voice tells us there are thirty seconds to go. (No static anymore: The D.V. has regained his composure.) *Yea, though I walk through the valley of the shadow of death.* Next to me, Eder is shaking even more.

Twenty seconds. *Thy rod and thy staff they comfort me.*

Until now, I have spent very little time on The Rock thinking about Eder. Maybe he has amused me a little or irritated me slightly. Mostly I have not paid much attention to him.

I feel sorry for him now. Eder is afraid. He thinks he is going to die. I have no idea what will happen at zero hour. I do not have a whole lot of confidence in the men running the show, but I have enough to believe I am going to live.

Eder is suffering and I do not want that to continue. I break the rules and I stop standing at attention. *Surely goodness and mercy shall follow me.* I reach out and touch Eder's arm. I want to stop the trembling. I want to let him know that both of us will be alive later. I imagine that my fingers—anyone's fingers—are capable of communicating that. Although, of course, I am not *really* imagining. Just doing. Just grabbing Eder's arm with my hand to steady him and let him know that somebody cares, even if it happens to be me.

I feel him begin to relax. I squeeze his arm and the shaking stops. And then I obey the rules and put my own arm at my side and stand at attention again.

H minus ten seconds. I am instructed now to raise up the arm that is at my side and place it over my closed eyes.

No sound but the countdown and our loud breathing. Five, Four, Three, Two, One. A buzzing noise.

6:25 A.M. I am alive. And so is Eder and everyone else.

At that moment, a wave of intense heat rolled over us. It felt like a tropical midday sun had just climbed into the sky, but this sun was much much hotter and brighter than any I had been under before. Even though I was facing away from the blast with an arm covering my closed eyes, the light was blinding me. I had never "felt" light before, but I did then. I could feel the light penetrating my arm and my eyelids.

When we were finally given permission to turn around and look, I saw nothing. I *was* blind, the way you are right after you stare at a very bright light, like a flashbulb. In seconds, I regained my vision and above and in front of me was a mushroom cloud. Oddly, it remained in place like a solid object stuck in the sky. The wind (if there was one) did not disperse it the way it did clouds I had watched in the past.

A full minute after zero hour, I heard the noise. Not the deafening sound I had expected but a distant rumble like thunder. Not loud, but there was no mistaking the power. The island trembled (like Eder) and it felt like there had just been an earthquake. Or a pilot had broken through the sound barrier again.

Then at last the mushroom cloud moved. Drifted over toward our island, threatening us a little, I thought, before finally heading north away from The Rock.

We did not find out until later that this was not the monster bomb that a plane was going to drop. We had witnessed a nuclear device with an energy yield of 40 kilotons (equivalent to forty thousand tons of TNT), a "miniature" hydrogen bomb or, as some of the newspapers called it, a "pocket-size" bomb. And yet this "miniature" device had just created a crater 400 feet wide and 55 feet deep at ground zero, a platform on the reef off Runit Island in Eniwetok Atoll.

Soon after we turned around and opened our eyes, we were allowed to depart and have breakfast. We went to the mess hall and that morning the watery coffee almost tasted good.

Then back to the barracks, where the men were exuberant. Relieved to be alive. A sense of invulnerability had taken over, and the volume was louder than the noisiest moments of the past. Radios, screaming and a discussion of the morning's entertainment.

"Big deal!" Billy Byrne said, almost yelling. Heads nodded in agreement.

"I don't know what the fuss was all about," Hawkins announced.

More nodding heads.

Eder was not doing push-ups. He was lying on the floor on his back. His first comment: "Boy, do I need a broad."

"What was all *that* about?" Straletti said.

"Damned if I know," Noonen responded. "I've seen better explosions in the movies."

At that moment, Eder jumped up off the floor. "I knew all the time there was nothing to worry about," he said with a new confidence. "I told you guys the army wasn't going to take any chances." He looked around at the men one by one. The star, center stage, speaking to his audience.

"You heard what Major Maxwell said," he continued. "Safety is the number one priority around here. They're not going to fool around with our lives. But some people never realized that. I can tell you, some guys were pretty nervous before the blast. They thought they weren't long for this world. And I know for a fact that one guy in particular was standing there pissing in his pants."

Eder swiveled his head, searching for the one guy. Then he looked at me and pointed. And everyone in the room stopped talking and turned and stared at me. They all waited to find out what Eder had to say. I of course waited too.

"Harris was scared shitless," Eder said, still pointing at me. "He was so nervous during the countdown that he had to grab my arm."

The silence slid out of the room and everyone looked at me and pointed at me and laughed.

I thought for a moment and decided I probably *had* been a bit nervous. Then I surprised myself and laughed too. "You could be right about that," I said to Eder. "Maybe I *was* scared."

The laughter started all over again, but this time I was included. This time they were laughing with me and not at me.

And I felt pretty good, considering the way I had spent the morning.

WILSON'S BROOM

RELIEF IN THE BARRACKS. EVERYBODY SURVIVED BLAST NUMBER ONE AND THAT meant there was nothing to worry about. And then Hawkins announced: "They've postponed the second test!"

"They never told us the second test was scheduled," Straletti pointed out.

"What do you think it means, Noonen?" Jason Underwood asked.

Noonen: "I can't worry about shit like that when my wife is making out with her next-door neighbor."

"She write you that?" Berko asked.

"Of course not. But I can read between the lines."

Berko: "You know what she's like, huh?"

"Fucking A!"

Berko: "She fools around a lot?"

"Not until now. But I can tell what's going on. She doesn't write what she's doing. Only how her parents are and what she eats. That tells me plenty."

Berko: "Have you ever met the neighbor?"

Noonen: "Of course not. She just moved into a new place. I don't even know who her neighbors are. But I can read between the lines, if you know what I mean."

"I think so," Berko said. "But I'm not sure."

"You're right about that," Noonen said, ending the conversation.

Three days later, Tony told us there was a second postponement.

"What's going on around here?" Eder asked. "Something must be wrong."

"If you want to know the truth, this is making me uncomfortable," Hawkins said.

"Me too," Billy Byrne repeated. Not just echoing words. He *looked* worried.

"Why so many postponements?" Straletti asked, and the response was a roomful of shrugs.

The third postponement was greeted with silence. Except from Jason Underwood: "Eder was right! There *is* something wrong."

"They never tell us *why* they keep postponing the test," Duncan said. "That's not a good sign."

"The major's been acting strange lately," Straletti said. "He walks around with his head down. And he doesn't seem to hear people when they talk to him."

"Such is life," said Richter, offering his poetic pronouncement.

"He's been snapping at people," Craig said. "More than usual. And I've noticed that sometimes his hands are shaking."

"That's not good," Billy Byrne said.

Straletti: "Twice I heard him walk up to someone and start a conversation. You know what he said? 'There's nothing to worry about.' Both times. Isn't that peculiar?"

"What does it mean?" Jason Underwood asked.

"It means *he's* very worried," Richter said. Once again offering us his psychoanalytic wisdom.

Richter was never shy about providing this kind of information, along with all the gory details of his own therapy. He claimed his Central Park West childhood was one continuous trauma because his mother walked around their apartment naked all day and kept him in a permanent state of arousal. He was now more determined than ever to be a psychoanalyst, he said. He loved sharing his insights with the rest of the world.

"The major's worried? That's interesting," Jason Underwood said.

"Interesting? Shit! Scary is what it is," said Hawkins.

Every few days we were told there was another delay—even though we had never been informed about a specific future date. Each time Major Maxwell announced an aborted shot, he seemed to be saying a nonexistent blast would not take place.

Worse, he never explained why this was happening. Or explained why he wasn't explaining. All he said was: "The game is patience. No reason to be upset."

"I told you what *that* means," Richter said. "It means *he's* upset."

"And the major knows what's going on," Eder said.

"That's what you think," Berko mumbled, but nobody heard him except me.

"If *he's* worried, we ought to be," said Billy Byrne.

"You're right," Craig said, and a few other men agreed. Billy Byrne smiled.

"And don't forget," Straletti reminded everyone, "the next test is The Big One. The first H-bomb ever dropped from a plane."

"What makes it big?" Jason Underwood asked.

"I don't know," Straletti said. "Maybe it's louder. Maybe the cloud is bigger."

"It's scary," Billy Byrne said. And then he looked over at Wilson, sweeping as usual. "But *he's* not worried. He's lucky. Nothing ever bothers him."

And so it seemed. Sweeping the floor next to his bed hour after hour. Body moving automatically without guidance from his brain. A rhythm in the steady brushing back and forth. He created a kind of music, gentle and intense.

Never speaking, never reacting to other men. Fading into the noise and mood of the barracks, part of the concrete. The expression, not sad or happy or lonely, never changes. Always blank. No look of pleasure or displeasure. No sign he desires or needs anything but the broom.

Invisible and ignored. You had to look hard to notice him. And when you did, you saw brown hair, glazed eyes (unalive) and the pale face of a ghost who never finds the sun. The eyes and the powdery pallor gave him the drab look of a lost man with prison years still in his head. Passing the time now in one of two ways: remembering or forgetting.

He was the sort of man, you never remembered what he looked like after you saw him. Not colorless but exuding the absence of color (like The Rock itself). He was opaque, making it easy to project anything onto him. Wilson was always whatever anyone wanted him to be.

And to Billy Byrne today he was irritating. "The sound of that broom gets to me sometimes."

Richter: "He's Ol' Man River, he just keeps rollin' along."

Billy Byrne glared at Wilson and shook his head. The look on Billy Byrne's face made it clear that for him the monotonous sweeping was getting louder and louder every minute. "Don't you ever stop?" he mumbled.

He didn't seem to realize he had said the words out loud until he heard his own voice. He looked around to check out the reactions of the other men. Instead of the usual disapproving faces, there was mild amusement. Eder nodded. Hawkins said: "You give it to 'im, Billy Byrne!"

With raised spirits, he focused on Wilson again. This time his voice (like the broom) became louder: "Stop!"

Friendly laughter surrounded Billy Byrne. Men looked up from their magazines and card games, eager for something to think about besides postponements.

Billy Byrne grinned. For a change, they were not reminding him he was fat. They were on his side.

Billy Byrne continued talking to Wilson: "You getting it clean? Is it as much fun as it looks?"

Wilson went on sweeping with no change in expression. No sign he heard Billy Byrne or that he even knew Billy Byrne existed.

Billy Byrne became more aggressive and moved next to Wilson. He yelled: "Sweep!"

Wilson stopped. Held the broom tightly in his right hand. His left arm fell to his side as he turned around. But he didn't look up. He stared at the floor. Showed no emotion.

Billy Byrne's eyes darted around the room searching for approval. Faces encouraged him and he talked to Wilson again: "Be useful for a change and clean up the rest of the barracks. Sweep the other rooms too."

A long wait. Then Billy Byrne started again: "You're not answering me and that's not polite." Silence. He moved his mouth close to Wilson's ear and shouted: "Polite! Polite!"

Wilson continued sweeping. A moment later he belched. A chorus of laughter surrounded him.

Billy Byrne: "You think about chow when you sweep! Repeat that for the West Coast audience!"

Billy Byrne put his hands in his pockets, felt a piece of paper, pulled out a laundry list. He crumpled it in his hand and dropped it on the floor. Then he moved to the door to watch.

Wilson examined the paper with suspicion. Was it alive? Would it move? He stared for a long time. Then with one swift swing of the long, round piece of wood in his hands, he swept the alien object into the hallway.

Excitement smothered the room. Talking stopped. Reading came to an end. Down went copies of *The Philadelphia Inquirer, The Amboy Dukes, Action Comics, Life* magazine. No more games, shoe-polishing, playing with Silly Putty, rolling tobacco, painting by the numbers. Everyone concentrated on two men.

It was time for the big bout, Billy Byrne vs. Wilson—the man they took for granted but now one of the headliners providing the entertainment. It was Billy Byrne they were rooting for because, let's face it, that's where the fun was going to be. Sure he's a creep and all he ever does is agree. And yes, he raises his eyebrows when he speaks and turns every sentence into an apology, but right now he knows how to spark the mood and amuse an audience.

Billy Byrne pulled a pack of gum from his pocket, ripped off the wrappers and stuffed each stick in his mouth one by one. Enormous wads forced into a small opening very quickly. He looked like Charlie Chaplin in a speeded-up film.

Then Billy Byrne dropped the crumpled gum wrappers in front of the broom. Wilson ignored them at first, bent down after a while, picked them up, put them in his pocket.

No sound except the noisy chomping of gum. A silent crowd waited for Billy Byrne. Seconds later, he walked over to Wilson's footlocker and opened it up. On top were Wilson's shirts. The laundry wasn't good enough for *his* shirts! After they were washed and pressed and returned, Wilson ironed them again. Billy Byrne took out a few and dropped them near the broom.

Wilson swept around them. As if he didn't notice. Then stopped. Glared at them. Picked them up. Casual and matter of fact.

Billy Byrne could feel the men with him, but still something was wrong. Wilson was not reacting. He was wearing a mask. On top of his neck, a head with an empty face. Billy Byrne needed to see *something* in those vacant eyes. He needed Wilson to be aware of him. Otherwise, Billy Byrne himself would not really be alive.

Wilson started to go back to his footlocker with the shirts. Billy Byrne stood in the way and blocked his path. Wilson stopped for a moment and the men confronted each other. Still no expression on Wilson's face. He did not even acknowledge Billy Byrne. Walked around him as if Billy Byrne were not there.

Billy Byrne turned to his audience: "I wonder what he'd do with sand. Would he put sand in his pocket? Why don't we find out?"

Billy Byrne was a leader. The king, and men were following his orders, doing what he wanted. They hurried to the shower room, grabbed the cleanup pails, tossed the mops stored inside onto the floor, carried the empty buckets to the lagoon, filled them with sand from the beach. A change of pace to keep Wilson from getting bored. And everyone else. No yawns this afternoon. Even the air was different. Heavy with excitement.

And me? A silent bystander. I didn't turn away. I didn't leave. I said nothing but I watched loudly.

Around me: rushing and blurred motion. Men filling pails, and they didn't know why, didn't know anything except this was a kick and the God damn bucket weighs a ton and my arm feels like it's falling off.

Wilson continued sweeping. The same small piece of floor over and over. Unintereoted in the activity around him.

Then events unfolded quickly. Hands reached inside full pails and grabbed fistfuls of sand. Arms stretched out. Fingers shook, waved, scattered. Spread apart and funneled grains onto the floor, and human hourglasses let the sand fall downward, flowing slowly, making thin layers and small piles on the concrete.

Wilson was maneuvered into a corner. He continued to move his broom back and forth but in a smaller area. The vacant expression remained.

Men carpeted the floor with sand. Then pulled back to the door (where I was standing) and watched.

Wilson was organized. He made separate piles in each corner of the room, one of them near his bed where he usually did all his sweeping. He combined four into two and then into one large pile in front of his bed, which he swept out of the floor-level aluminum window. All the time he remained silent. It took ten minutes but the room was finally clean again. Then the regular sweeping began, over and over as before. As if nothing had ever happened.

Billy Byrne: "Sand is too easy. How about mud?"

Others joined in: "Yes! How about mud!"

Finally a chorus of agreement: "Mud!"

This time buckets of water were lugged from the shower room along with more sand from the beach. Everything organized, with a few leaders assigning men to pails and directing traffic and pointing out where to put the pails. Chaos carefully arranged.

They emptied the buckets onto the floor. Tossed sand around the room and splashed water on top, spraying themselves. Mixed everything together with their shoes, going at it like little kids, stamping and grinding mud into the cement, rubbing it in everywhere.

Off with the shoes. Jumping up and down barefoot. Hey, this is great, and men on all fours spreading the mud around, using arms and knees and toes and elbows to coat the floor. Lying down and rolling, letting clothes and skin soak it all up, turning clean khakis and clean flesh brown.

Fingers: grabbing, flinging, hurling, tossing, splattering. Greedy hands reaching out and slinging brown shit. Mud pies make everyone forget who they are and where they are. Pores hungry for dirt after days and weeks and months of cleaning themselves and the rest of the island, and Hey, Man, I haven't enjoyed myself this much since I got here.

Everything sloppy and here's mud in your eye and nose and mouth, brown lumps for making soft shapes. Hitting targets brings to the faces of men sudden expressions of friendly surprise with white teeth caught flashing from ear to ear and looking whiter against the mud.

But messing up the room is not enough. Don't forget Wilson. His clean clothes, carefully washed and doubly pressed, were too neat and they had to do something about that. Wilson The Clean was an enemy. One of those closed-up people standing in the way of freedom.

A new frenzy took over and busy hands covered Wilson's white face and clean khakis with mud. Hundreds of fingers rubbed him with mud until he was black. Big Mammy on the poster finally had company.

Then the room quieted down. Suddenly. And the men waited to see what Wilson was going to do now.

Wilson looked at the floor and into the eyes of each man one at a time. He held the broom at an angle and looked at each man. Grabbed the tip of the broom handle with his two hands and rested his chin on top.

Then the men stopped being in the room for him. He stared into space. Far away. Perceiving in dimensions different from what the rest of us could comprehend. He stayed in the middle of the room, leaning on his broom and staring. From time to time he looked around at the mud.

And quietly he cried. Emotion for the first time. No noise. No sound at all. No sobbing, but from time to time a tear moved down his cheek and cleared a path along his muddy face.

An hour later he came out of the mood. He was himself again. He filled a bucket with water and began the long task of scrubbing.

CODE NAME: CHEROKEE

THE SECOND TEST. MONDAY, MAY 21, 1956—SIXTEEN DAYS AFTER WE watched the "pocket-size" hydrogen fusion bomb. Another early morning wake-up, but this time we knew we were going to see the big one. Code name: Cherokee.

The press had watched and reported on the opening act and (along with us) waited impatiently through eight postponements for the main event. They were finally going to get what they had come for. And so were we. We were all going to see the monster explode.

Another march to the lagoon. Another morning to hurry up and wait, to stand at attention and at ease. Another countdown with the disembodied voice, with an arm over closed eyes and no goggles.

Today, Eder and Noonen and Hawkins and Underwood were not afraid they were going to die—they said they were going to write home about this one. Friends and family might not have a "need to know," but what could be wrong with telling them what they've already read on the front pages of their newspapers?

Still, they were tense. They had never figured out what a very large bomb was going to be like, and they didn't know if they should be excited or nervous. They seemed both.

I stood there (at attention and at ease) and thought about words we had heard many times from Major Maxwell (reading from his script).

"It takes six hundred roentgens to kill a man. Everyone is exposed to roentgens every day from the sun and the earth. We will receive only a small number from the blast. There is no danger to anyone. Repeat: no danger!"

"Repeat" was one of the major's favorite words. Richter said it was a counterindicator. "Repeat: no danger!" meant Better Watch Out.

5:51 A.M. Zero hour.

With no goggles and my eyes closed, I was blind to the giant fireball that rose with incredible speed, leaving the earth behind. I could not watch an immense pillar of fire rise from the ground in pursuit less than a second later, catch up, and then appear to push the fireball higher and higher into the sky. I did not observe them racing together for another twenty seconds until the pillar vanished behind clouds and the fireball dimmed and disappeared. I learned about the sights I did not see in the same way as the rest of the world: I read about them in the newspapers.

When we were finally permitted to open our eyes and look, I watched a giant cloud spread out and up and take over the sky until I was sure that nothing else remained in the universe. At first this mushroom was partially obscured by other, ordinary clouds, all of them gray, but soon it freed itself and emerged in iridescent colors: deep purple on the bottom to pale orange and then pink on top. This enormous hood kept expanding in every direction, and eventually the mushroom cloud became a hundred miles wide and reached a height of twenty-five miles. The other sun rose forty-two minutes later and looked puny compared to the one that had just filled the sky.

The reporters were excited by what they had seen and wrote that Cherokee was the experience of a lifetime (borrowing MM's words). But they were going home. We would have many more experiences of a lifetime and we had no idea how they were going to turn out.

The newspapermen wrote that they would never be able to forget that explosion. We felt the same way but for another reason. Something happened that morning that the press was not going to learn about for another twenty-five days.

The story first appeared in *The Honolulu Star-Bulletin* on June 15. An informant identified only as "a test technician" told the paper that the May 21 hydrogen bomb had missed its target.

The intended ground zero was directly over Namu Island, but the flight crew mistook an observation facility on a different island for their targeting beacon and the bomb detonated "considerably off target" over the ocean northeast of Namu.

In military jargon: The weapon delivery was grossly in error and all of the weapons effects data were lost.

In plain English: The United States was not going to get one bit of information from this particular test. It was a waste of time and many many millions of dollars and (as I will soon explain) thousands of eyes.

Donald A. Quarles, secretary of the air force, confirmed the *Star-Bulletin* story the next day and admitted the mistake was "due to human error."

So there it was for everyone to see and know. The first time the United States dropped an H-bomb from a plane, we hit the wrong target.

Berko came up with a solution: "Give the pilot more practice dropping H-bombs!"

Later that summer *The New York Times* reported that, after an investigation, the air force identified "the test technician" as Airman First Class Jackson H. Kilgore, a helicopter mechanic, and sent him to Eniwetok, where he was arrested for disclosing classified information. He remained "in custody" while the local commander decided if a court-martial was justified, and eventually Kilgore was released with only a reprimand. He became a free man. Where? *On duty at Eniwetok.*

Berko and I wondered what would have happened to him if he had been found guilty.

But enough of Airman Kilgore. It's time to get back to the eyes.

Before Cherokee, we all faced the lagoon. The explosion was going to be behind us. The major reminded us that this was essential, as he had done so many times before. Face the blast, he said, and our eyes could be damaged permanently, even if they were closed.

And not just our eyes. Although he never did get specific about what other body parts might be affected.

The disembodied voice repeated the warning again and again over the loudspeaker.

"Don't turn around before the countdown reaches zero.

"Don't turn around after the countdown reaches zero.

"Don't turn around until you are told it is safe to turn around."

We stood at attention. And paid attention. Lined up as instructed. Backs to the ocean. Following orders. Careful to avoid permanent damage.

The countdown and the disembodied voice. "Four, three, two, one, zero."

The flash of light.

The low distant rumble.

The shaking of the earth.

And guess what? The pilot missed the target, but our eyes hit the target. We didn't have to turn around after thirty seconds. The fireball and the mushroom cloud were right there in front of us. We goggleless enlisted men were facing ground zero. A result of pilot error.

How do you react to this?

You want to get even—an eye for an eye. But there's no one to blame. And what good will anger do anyway? Little pieces of you will be eaten away (although that could happen anyway).

A few ragged thoughts enter your head. You open your eyes and you are glad you can still see. Then you think about how many days you have left on the island. The magic number. Mine is eighty-one, but there is a chance it might be eighty-two since 1956 is a leap year. That number is the only escape from this moment and this island.

You remember the warning: "Face the blast and you'll have permanent eye damage." You feel better when you realize the source for this particular piece of information. But Major Maxwell was only reading from his well-known sheets of paper, and who knew where they came from and how accurate they were.

If what he was saying was incorrect, that meant *his* superiors didn't know what the fuck they were talking about, and you were in real trouble. But if he was right, you could feel secure knowing you were in the hands of capable people who didn't make mistakes. And that meant it was only a matter of time before all of us went blind.

Thoughts like that could give anyone headaches. So you try to erase them before they form. You stop thinking. Mental contraception. You have to lose your mind (or else you'll lose your mind).

You don't talk about what happened. And everyone finds it easy to remain silent. The posters and the speeches remind you never to discuss anything unless it is on a "need to know" basis. Many men are afraid to express opinions. Afraid, even, to have opinions.

You pretend nothing unusual took place and you are almost able to convince yourself it was just your imagination. That can make the next blast easier. You don't have to fill up your head ahead of time wondering where *that* explosion will be coming from.

So you feel the initial shock. On the ground. In the sky. In your head. What follows is a calmness. A feeling of profound detachment. A bizarre kind of numbness.

You realize you will have to wait and see.

Wait and see if you can still see later.

THE GREATEST
WEATHER-FORECASTING
SYSTEM IN HISTORY

———————— ⚛ ————————

MANY DAYS AFTER CHEROKEE, WE WERE ALL ASSEMBLED FOR AN IMPORTANT AN-
nouncement from Major Maxwell. We knew before he started that it
would have nothing to do with the pilot error. *We* weren't talking
about it. No chance MM would.

He squinted his eyes, cleared his throat and gave us one of his
I'm-disappointed-in-you expressions. "How often do I have to say this?
Around here, it's safety first, second and third. We absitively posolutely
never take chances."

As always, it took a while to figure out just where he was heading.

"I've gotten reports about low morale. I've heard some of you
have been worried because we had a few postponements. It's hard to
believe you think anything could go wrong at Joint Task Force Seven.
I'm here to tell you to stop thinking. Yes, we had delays, and now I'm
going to tell you why. The reason is simple."

And very old news. Before Cherokee, we were all concerned but we
had already found out what the problem was. Unfavorable Weather

Conditions. We got the information from our reliable Stateside sources, the letters from home. Reporters on the *Mount McKinley* wrote many articles on this very subject, which were printed in our local newspapers, and even though the mail took forever to reach us, the clippings had been in our back pockets for a while.

"Use your think tank," MM said loud and clear, a direct order. "And think weather. We have a terrific team working hard to make *your* life better. At Weather Central, fourteen forecasters and twenty-five observers are collecting and correlating data twenty-five hours a day. Just for you. Ten reconnaissance planes fly at least two missions a day within twelve hundred miles of Eniwetok and give us data about winds, clouds, temperature, relative humidity and rain from sea level up to thirty thousand feet."

As usual, the major's eyes were focused on those familiar sheets of paper. He turned a page and continued.

"We're careful with a capital K. Planes reconnoiter storms and typhoons to warn us about impending high winds, and they gather information right up to the moment of the blast. We insist on ideal conditions, and we don't move forward unless the weather is perfect. If necessary, we'll cancel a test one second before zero hour."

At this moment, MM was actually reassuring me. Which I had never thought possible. I remembered Castle Bravo, a test that could have been postponed but wasn't. Maybe they *did* learn a lesson. Whoever "they" were.

MM: "We take every precaution and make sure nothing can go wrong." The very thought of a mistake made the major deliver one of his isn't-that-ridiculous laughs. The chuckle, the throat-clearing, the nodding, and he was ready to continue. "We never take chances. Not with the weather. Not with anything else. Around here there is no danger." He paused and looked around. And then added: "Repeat: no danger."

Richter rolled his eyes.

"Now I'm really going to impress you," the major told us. "I'm going to let you know how many weather stations we have supplying data to us and where they are all located. Eight on islands near Eniwetok and Bikini, two in the Fiji Islands, the Hawaiian Islands, Japan, the Aleutian Islands, Iwo Jima, Okinawa, Formosa, the Philippines,

Guam, Indonesia, Hong Kong, Singapore, New Guinea, Marcus and Darwin, Australia."

Marcus?

Jason Underwood, pencil and paper in hand, jotted down the name of each location. Or tried to. He wasn't able to scribble fast enough.

The major turned the page: "As a result of all this we can predict weather conditions in the upper atmosphere over the Pacific Proving Ground with greater accuracy than ever before. We can also prevent radioactive fallout in all populated areas. Thanks to Weather Central, you'll be in the pink of health thirty years from now telling your grandchildren about the exciting experiences you had during Operation Redwing."

This was not the first time on The Rock I had received assurances about the state of my health decades into the future. My silent reaction was always the same: The United States had dropped atomic bombs on Hiroshima and Nagasaki less than eleven years before, so no one—not even Major Maxwell—could know how any of us were going to be affected by radiation fifteen, twenty or thirty years after exposure. Confident statements to the contrary made me question the intelligence of the speaker. Particularly at this moment.

"What we're accomplishing now would have been unheard-of even a year ago. We've assembled The Greatest Weather-Forecasting System in History, and that means there is no possibility that winds can carry a radioactive cloud to this island. Take my word for it: There will never be fallout on Eniwetok."

It was 1956, and Major Maxwell was making two guarantees. We were going to have Accurate Weather Forecasting and Safe H-Bomb Tests.

THE F WORD

TWO TESTS FOR THE PRICE OF ONE.

Zuni (on Bikini Atoll) and Yuma (on Eniwetok), numbers three and four, took place the next day two hours apart. Named, as usual, after American Indian tribes.

The Zuni device was developed by UCRL (the University of California Radiation Laboratory) and called Bassoon—named, like all their others, after birds or musical instruments. Why identify destructive weapons in this oddly lyrical way? I never heard a sensible explanation. I wondered if some UCRL scientist liked the music of woodwinds and canaries.

Zuni's ground zero was Eninman Island, also known as Tare, and Yuma's was Aomon, also known as Sally. Every island had two names—the first the native Marshall Islands name, the second created by the military "to prevent confusion." A goal that was not achieved.

Yuma had a yield of 0.19 kilotons and was tiny compared to Zuni's 3.5 megatons (almost as big as Cherokee with 3.8). And yet they appeared to be the same size to those of us watching on Eniwetok Island. The reason: Ground zero for the larger bomb was so much farther away. Often it was impossible to tell just by looking if the bomb du jour was a monster.

Two shots in two hours. We told each other we were under attack, although we didn't realize that was literally true until a few hours after the second countdown. That was when we encountered the F word. I'm not talking about the four-letter Anglo-Saxon blockbuster, an F word that on Eniwetok you can only dream about. I'm referring to the F word that wasn't a dream but a nightmare.

There was posolutely no danger of fallout. It can't happen—and certainly not here. Not with The Greatest Weather-Forecasting System in History. So what went wrong? A sudden "unexpected" shift in the winds.

I never did find out which of the two explosions was responsible or if it was both of them. But I first became aware of what was going on halfway through a rainy morning when our old friend, the Disembodied Voice, made an announcement over the loudspeaker outside the supply depot.

"Everyone go indoors. At once!" the D.V. ordered. "It is imperative for your safety that you get inside the nearest building right away and remain there. You must make certain that all the doors and all the windows are closed."

Please notice that the F word was never once used.

We all realized the D.V. had undergone a major transformation. During countdowns, he was casual, relaxed and matter of fact. Now we heard a different tone: an unmistakable sense of urgency that was alarming.

He repeated the warning. Repeated it again. And then again. He made it abundantly clear that absolutely nobody would be allowed to remain outdoors under any circumstances. (Did it ever occur to him that absolutely nobody would *want* to?) Over and over. Everyone HAD TO BE inside. With doors and windows shut. For our own safety.

There was one more indication this was not going to be your run-of-the-mill morning in the tropics. The rain was making a clicking noise when the drops landed on the radiological survey meter outside the depot. That meant the water was radioactive. If the radiation level should increase, the clicks would become louder and more frequent. As we discovered starting with that morning, the sound and the downpour went together. In 1956, there was never a fallout on Eniwetok without rain—as far as we knew.

At this moment, the clicking was steady and the D.V. repeated his warning yet again: "Everyone go indoors. At once!" he said in a tinny, echoing voice. "It is imperative for your safety that you get inside the nearest building right away and remain there. You must make certain that all the doors and all the windows are closed."

The repetition and the unmistakably urgent tone of the D.V.'s voice underlined the gravity of the situation. "Imperative for your safety," the D.V. kept stressing. "Close all the windows."

Was this a joke? Some kind of cosmic screwup? *None* of the aluminum windows would close at the supply depot (or in other buildings on the island). Corrosion and rust and broken hinges made it impossible to shut any of them. The windows were permanently and unalterably "locked" into an open position.

Close the windows? Yeah. Right.

All of us remained at our desks except for Joel Estabrook, who jumped up from his chair, ran over to the side of the building and tried to close the window.

Imperative for your safety.

Estabrook had a round face that barely needed shaving and (like Duncan) looked no older than fourteen. But he was twenty-one with a wife and two children and, after he graduated from high school in Colorado, he became a full-time gardener.

"You just got here," Berko told Estabrook, still struggling with the window. "Wait until you've been around for a while. You'll find out you're wasting your time with shit like that. It's a hopeless cause."

Estabrook ignored the remark. Sweating and cursing, he continued trying to pull the window toward him and close it.

"What is this shit?" he shouted at everyone and no one as he tugged and yanked at the window that wouldn't budge. "This fucker doesn't move!"

"Be careful," Berko said, "or else you'll break it."

Estabrook started to hit the aluminum with his fists: "Close, you motherfucker," he shouted, pounding on the window. His hands began to bleed.

The steady clicking outside continued and so did the D.V.'s warnings. Major Vanish was doing his usual number: staring off into space. Captain Weiss looked concerned but he was silent. They both ignored Estabrook. And Major Vanish displayed no sign at all that he even heard the D.V. and the clicking.

Good old Straletti was also staring into space. Silent. Apparently unaware.

A couple of other men talked about last night's movie. Which was terrible as always. They sounded like they were surprised about that.

Eder was telling us how much he wanted to get laid.

Meanwhile, Estabrook moved to another window, tried to pull that one closed and failed again. He began hammering the window with his bleeding hands. "Motherfucker!" he screamed. "God damn motherfucker! Back home they're building God damn underground atomic bomb shelters everywhere. Where the fuck is ours?"

"Hey, Estabrook!" Berko yelled. "Why don't you put through a requisition for new windows? Maybe they'll get here in time for the next series of tests."

"Fuck you!" Estabrook shouted.

"Why don't you go outside and try to push the window in?" Berko suggested. "It'll be easier to close that way."

In response, Estabrook picked up his typewriter and threw it at the window. (I expected him to hurl it at Berko.)

The captain said sternly: "Enough of that!" Another clear indication this was no run-of-the-mill morning. Mere conversation was strictly verboten on other days.

Estabrook, suddenly subdued, said: "Yes, sir." He picked up his typewriter (amazingly unbroken) and, defeated for the moment, went back to his desk.

The clicking continued and so did the warning to close the windows.

I looked over at Estabrook. His eyes were wet but I knew he was not going to cry because men didn't do that on Eniwetok. Except Billy Byrne. And Wilson once.

Estabrook began to talk. To himself? To everyone? To no one? "They treat you like shit out here," he said. "I never volunteered to come to this fucking place. I don't want to be fried by radiation, but I had nothing to say about it. They drafted me, but that doesn't give them the right to set off H-bombs around me and use me as a human guinea pig. The army and the government, they don't give a damn about us. I hate them. I'm ashamed of my country. I'm ashamed to be American."

He might as well have been speaking to a group of deaf men. Absolutely no one seemed to be listening except for me and, as it turned out, Eder.

Eder, Mr. Patriot, didn't like hearing his country insulted and he responded predictably. He walked over to Estabrook and punched him in the gut. "Shut the fuck up," he said.

Estabrook doubled over, then straightened up and was about to slam his own fist into a person and not an aluminum window. About to, but he was stopped. Not by a human being. By silence.

The clicking was over.

A moment later the D.V. gave us permission to open the windows again.

ASSES AND ELBOWS

"WE'VE GOT A SERIOUS PROBLEM HERE," MAJOR VANISH TOLD US A HALF HOUR later. "We're going to do something about it right now."

He had everyone's attention. And not just because it was one of the few times we had ever heard him speak.

He explained: "The supply depot is filthy, inside and out. We're going to change that."

A dirt crisis! A situation this serious required the extraordinary measures he was now taking—he combined two important depot institutions, the Daily Cleanup Period and the Saturday Inspection. Precedent-shattering, since this was a weekday and not Saturday and we had already cleaned up the office once that morning.

Our first destination was the closet at the front of the building where brooms, dustpans and rags were stored. And distributed, as always, in a military manner with great formality. Next we swept the floor, cleaned and dusted typewriters, emptied wastebaskets and arranged papers on desks in neat stacks.

Then we lined up in single file for the march outside to clean up our concrete garden, already in pristine condition. We were required to pick up cigarette butts and scraps of paper that weren't there—unfortunately, Major Vanish had instituted a quota system and insisted that each of us produce at least five pieces. Before we were allowed back inside, we had to open up our clenched fists to make certain they were clutching the proper amount of refuse.

Just as we were about to make our exit, I noticed small shells and pieces of coral on Estabrook's desk. Just what I needed to fill my quota, so I grabbed a handful (at least five).

"What are you doing!" Estabrook wanted to know. "I've been collecting those for my wife. I thought they would look pretty in her greenhouse."

I apologized, embarrassed that I had almost made his already difficult day even worse. Fortunately, Berko heard us and handed me some cigarette butts that he kept in his pocket permanently for just these occasions.

Outside, Major Vanish barked out his orders: "If it isn't aluminum or concrete, pick it up! I don't want to see anything but asses and elbows!" More proof that his vocal cords were not permanently impaired.

When he wasn't looking, I dropped my newly acquired butts on the ground and picked them up when he turned around.

Back inside, Major Vanish checked out our office equipment—the inspection usually reserved for Saturdays. We stood at our desks as he marched down the aisle and examined all the typewriters on his left. Then he made a return trip in the other direction and looked at the rest. At these moments, he maintained his customary silence. He glared and pointed at offending dirt, which he then touched with a forefinger before scowling. Rust brought an expression of even greater disgust.

But the dirt and the rust were figments of his imagination and, like the butts we picked up, not actually there. We pretended otherwise. We attacked the nonexistent specks and went through the motions of eradicating them.

I knew Captain Weiss had to be embarrassed by this, but he was too professional to show it. He didn't flinch after Major Vanish delivered his own personal all-clear signal. The captain just went back to work like the rest of us.

While Major Vanish sat at his desk surveying his domain with the satisfied look of a man who had coped successfully with the crisis of the day.

FUSION CUISINE

―――――――――――――――⚛――――――――――――――――

"We're having a blast today." That was what they said at college before the Saturday night parties. Today we were having another kind of party. Blast number five with the code name Erie. A three-hundred-foot-high tower burst of a "clean" thermonuclear bomb at Runit (Yvonne) on Eniwetok Atoll. This would be the second time that island was ground zero, and it would not be the last. Poor little Runit would take it in the chops during Operation Redwing.

When I opened my eyes after zero hour, I saw the shock wave coming—a clear, massive, rippling cloud that looked like someone had crinkled up a huge roll of cellophane and was pulling it toward us with enormous force and speed. I was hit by a wind so powerful that it pushed back the skin on my face and almost blew me off my feet. An intense wave of suffocating heat rolled over me and made me feel my skin was on fire. For a moment, I was almost unable to breathe.

Today the sky was black and stars were shining, but artificial daylight made the island bright. A world that is light and dark at the same time. How can that be?

Jason Underwood, standing next to me, said the light reminded him of the glare from a welding rod. I took his word for it. I was a city boy who had never seen a welding rod.

I stared at my fingers and saw the bones in my hands. And then my arms. And my legs. I wasn't a person anymore. I was a skeleton. The test was Erie, and eerie it was. The H-bomb was X-raying me! And Jason Underwood too. I looked over and saw *his* bony fingers.

In front of me I watched a milky, simmering lagoon, water that seemed to be boiling. I thought about the deformed fish and wondered if they cared. They were probably used to it by now. Maybe they even liked it. Or maybe they felt nothing. I hoped I was not going to end up that way.

In the distance, a thin white wisp turned into the mushroom shape, and inside I saw lightning and all the colors of the spectrum. Finally, the enormous cloud spread out in every direction, obliterating the sky and obliterating my sense of space and time and identity.

After we were dismissed, Eder walked over to me. "It gets pretty boring," he said and sighed deeply. "You seen one H-bomb, you seen them all." Then he moved on quickly. Obviously hungry and in a hurry to get to the mess hall.

I headed there myself at a slower pace, and Jason Underwood tagged along. He asked me how come everyone on The Rock was still alive when hundreds of thousands of Japanese were killed in 1945 by bombs much less powerful than the ones we were testing.

I explained that the people who died were at or near ground zero, and if we had been on Runit Island before dawn, we wouldn't be having our conversation.

"That's a relief," Jason Underwood said as we reached the mess hall and the long line outside that ran the length of the building at every meal. He touched his face, a habit of his whenever he was deep in thought, and rubbed the distinctive brown mole on his right cheek—large but not disfiguring or even unattractive.

Finally he spoke again. "I guess we don't have anything to worry about, since they haven't dropped a bomb on us."

I was unable to restrain myself. "Yet," I replied, sounding to myself like Berko.

Jason Underwood's usual blank look told me he didn't get it. Which was just as well.

He was silent for a while. Then suddenly he spoke to me again: "You know, I've heard a lot of guys complain about the food out here, but I don't think it's so bad."

"Is that true?"

"I never lie," he told me, and as soon as he said it, I knew that was so. "The food's better than I used to get at home."

"What did you get at home?"

"Collard greens. Pig's knuckles. Mostly food the darkies eat—and not much of it. Now I can have all I want. Though to tell you the truth, it's not as good here as it was at Fort Bragg."

He inspected his uniform. "It's nice, too, to have clothes without any holes. And shoes. I didn't have them when I was growing up. I never saw a pair of sneakers before I got into the army."

The line moved ahead and he walked forward the same way he always did: head down, eyes on the floor.

Then he turned to me and gave me a sweet smile. "Some things are better here and some things aren't. You know, before I got to The Rock, I was a talkative person. More like I am today."

I detected a sparkle on his face.

"I'm hungry," he told me. "I can hardly wait for breakfast." Another smile.

I looked at his eyes. They weren't dead—I hadn't realized that before.

Just wounded.

I thought about test number five while I waited for breakfast, and I could almost understand why Eder had been so blasé and nonchalant—Erie had been uneventful (except for the special effects). A major relief and a big change.

Inside the mess hall there was a big change too, but I didn't notice it until Eder, just finished with breakfast, came over to me again.

"See, everything's different here this morning," he said.

I looked around and tried to figure out what he was talking about. The ambience was definitely the same, an improvement over a riot, considerably worse than a zoo. The clanking of the metal trays and the yelling were so loud that men standing or sitting next to each other had to shout to be heard.

Today, as always, the meals were served cafeteria-style, and the cooks, who were also the servers, slopped the food into compartments on the trays and sloshed lukewarm canned punch into unbreakable plastic cups. The hygiene was consistent with the cuisine: scores of tables, each seating four, were never cleared of crumbs or scraps of food (which also carpeted the floor).

I could tell with one glance that the quality of the food was no different—which was going to suit Jason Underwood just fine. I personally longed for the snack bar, which was better but not open for breakfast. I had already put myself on the Noonen diet at lunch and dinner: candy bars and Coke. But for culinary and not paranoid reasons.

I had no idea what Eder was referring to until he pointed at the servers. "Look," he said. "They're using Geiger counters today!"

And so they were. As I approached the food, I observed for the first time that the servers were indeed running Geiger counters over our breakfast before we dined.

"The army is playing it safe," Eder explained to me, again in one of his patriotic moods. "They're not taking any chances." And then he disappeared out of the mess hall.

While I waited to get to the front of the line, another batch of eggs was brought out from the kitchen. Which the server didn't check for radiation.

One of the men ahead of me yelled out: "Hey, use the Geiger counter!"

The server responded by throwing the serving spoon at him—and missing. It landed on the floor in a pool of sand, spilled food and a repulsive brown liquid. The soldier picked it up and flung it back at the cook, who ducked. The spoon landed in the eggs. He dished them out. No one objected.

Berkowitz, way in front of me, was taking his tray to a table and had a bite before he got there. "Better today than usual," he announced to everyone within hearing range, which happened to include me. "Nothing like a little radiation to give a meal that special gourmet touch."

THE MRS. BERKOWITZ DIET

CARL DUNCAN DID NOT SHARE EDER'S CASUAL ATTITUDE ABOUT THE TESTS OR feel as pleased about the new mess hall regimen. He told me the Geiger counter freaked him out.

"You can't take it too seriously. It's strictly routine," I told him, although I had personally found the powdered eggs hard enough to swallow under the old system. More difficult now.

I borrowed a few words from Eder: "The army is playing it safe. They're not taking any chances."

"You're just trying to make me feel better."

"That's true."

"Do you think it's safe on The Rock?" he asked. "Aren't you a little worried?"

"More than a little. It's dangerous here, but there's nothing we can do about it. Except try and adjust."

"Are you still staying out of the water?" he asked.

I nodded. "It's a decision I've made for myself. That doesn't mean *you* shouldn't swim every day the way you always have."

"No, it doesn't mean that," he agreed.

But I noticed he didn't go in the water that afternoon.

Tony insisted the tests and the fallout weren't getting to him. He was more than pleased that Irene loved her job as a registered nurse, the one that had been her first choice. He was a simple organism, he said, and if she was happy, so was he. His earliest childhood memory was being with Irene in a park while she told him he was special (the only one in the family who ever did). Beginning then, she had been there for him—mischievous, fun to be with, caring, loyal, bright. He said she deserved every break she got.

Maybe he *was* happy, but he *looked* terrible. Worn out and weary. Thinner. Face drawn. The sparkle in his eyes gone. The golden luster dimmed.

After a little prodding, I found out he was having heart palpitations and he was short of breath for hours at a time. So I told him the obvious—what I had once wanted him to say to me: "Why don't you see a doctor?" There were now three working at our hospital and dispensary.

Tony shrugged his shoulders. "There's nothing wrong with me. It would be a waste of everyone's time."

He was stubborn, so there was no point in arguing with him, but I wondered if he *was* sick. Or was it possible Redwing was affecting him more than he realized?

Berko also noticed Tony didn't look like himself. "You need a special treat," Berko told him. And he gave Tony the latest box of his mother's cookies—which seemed to arrive daily, although that, of course, was impossible since we didn't get mail that often. "Eat them all if you want. Give what's left over to the other guys."

Tony loved them. He gave Berko one of his rare smiles.

And he was not Mrs. Berkowitz's only fan. More than once, men were known to have proposed a toast or two to her before chug-a-lugging their beers at the Snakepit. Genuine atomic cookies.

Although I didn't hate them as much as Berko, I had to be pretty hungry to eat one.

Not surprisingly, Mrs. Berkowitz was very fat (I saw pictures of her). Her son, on the other hand, was very thin and got that way, I assumed, by never eating anything his mother baked. The Mrs. Berkowitz Diet.

"Why did she keep on making you cookies when you never ate them?" I asked.

"Because she didn't know I hated them."

"Didn't she notice that your dessert plate was always full?"

"Of course not. I hid that shit on my lap."

"And what did you end up doing with it?"

"Sometimes I turned the cakes and cookies into crumbs. Sometimes I didn't. But I always fed that crap to the pigeons. Thanks to my mother, America's fattest pigeons live in Brooklyn."

I smiled. "Won't the guys out here get fat eating her stuff?"

Berkowitz kept a straight face. "Of course not. They're going to turn into pigeons."

The first time I heard about Mrs. Berkowitz was on the plane to Eniwetok. "An island without women!" he said to me. "That's a laugh considering the promise I made to my mother before I left the States. She wanted me to swear to her I would never go out with a girl who wasn't Jewish."

"Have you *ever* gone out with a girl who wasn't Jewish?"

"All the time. I've been going out with Stephanie for as long as I can remember, and she's a shiksa."

"Your mother never met her?"

"She met her all the time. Steph lives in our apartment building in Brooklyn. And has since I was four years old."

"When did you start dating her?"

"When Steph and I were both thirteen."

"And your mother never noticed?"

"She was too busy baking," Berko said.

"So she didn't know you'd been going out with a girl who wasn't Jewish when she made you promise not to?"

"That's right. My mother only brought up the subject because I was leaving Brooklyn. Leaving the whole damn country. She was playing it safe."

"Are you going to keep your promise after you get back?" I asked.

"Of course."

"You mean you're never going to see Stephanie again?"

"I didn't say that. I'm never going to *date* Stephanie again. Ever."

"What's the difference?"

"Stephanie's got a husband now, so I *can't* date her."

"I don't understand."

"My mother doesn't know it, but the day before I left the States, Stephanie and I got married."

Berkowitz waited for me to react, but I was speechless—not the only occasion he had put me into that state, although this time I was more silent than usual. I remained that way as I contemplated his situation and wondered what the fireworks would be like when his mother found out. Which had not yet happened after all these months.

Would she stop sending cookies to her son and end her reign as an Eniwetok superstar?

I also wondered if Stephanie baked.

PART FOUR

The One-Year Paid Vacation

GLOWING TOENAILS AND
MUTATED COCONUTS

⚛

That evening Carl Duncan asked me to go to the Snakepit with him.

Thanks but no thanks. "I'm going to write a few letters at the depot," I told him. I liked spending quiet evenings there whenever I could. Which was most of the time.

I was surprised by Carl's invitation—I didn't think of him as a drinking buddy. I liked him. I even envied him a little because he was so certain about Penny and had known from the age of fourteen that she was the one for him.

I loved Nancy plenty, but our relationship was not that simple. She wanted to get married and I was not ready. At the age of fourteen, I was still coping with an endless childhood. I thought of my freshman year at college as the beginning of my life. By my calculations, that made me six years old, much too young to even *think* about marriage.

But I still spent all my time thinking about *Nancy*. And writing her, which I planned to do that evening.

My father too, though letters to him were difficult for me. He was a man of extremes. For fourteen years he ignored me. For the rest of his life, he worried about me too much.

He had never fully recovered from the death of his own parents within months of each other when he was sixteen. His father was a judge in Brooklyn and brought him up in an educated home. When my father's parents died, he was left penniless and quit high school to support himself in a variety of jobs. After my mother's death, he grieved for three people. Four including himself.

That never changed. He never dated—he said no one could replace my mother, a person I was not allowed to mention. He feared constantly that someday I would surprise him too and join the other three deceased members of his family. He showed his concern by displaying alarm even when I caught a cold.

So each time I wrote him, I was careful to not let him know what the island was *really* like. I sent pleasant, tranquil letters that never revealed what was happening to us. With Nancy, I was more candid, but I also tried to not upset *her.* Mail censorship *was* self-imposed.

But my best-laid plans for the evening were disrupted when Carl Duncan continued to press me about going to the Snakepit with him. He reminded me I had to walk past it on my way to the depot. So why didn't I drop in for a few minutes with him since I was going by anyway?

Again thanks but no thanks. I told him: "I don't drink anymore." I had gone on the wagon permanently when I realized that alcohol made me very depressed on The Rock.

"I don't drink either," Carl said. He told me he had never even tasted liquor or beer in the States (heresy for a Wisconsin man), and he had no intention of starting. Ever. On or off The Rock.

"Then why are you going to the Snakepit?" I surprised myself with the question. Men on the island were always doing strange things, and I had learned over time that the best policy was never to ask anyone "Why" about anything.

"To visit some friends. I'd like you to meet them." And he reminded me again that I wouldn't be going out of my way.

So I agreed. And two teetotalers joined the boozers at the local pub. What Carl didn't tell me was that his friends had four legs.

. . .

A dozen dogs roamed The Rock, mongrels vaguely resembling long-haired terriers. At night, they hung out at the Snakepit because the drinkers were generous with food and affection. And so was non-drinker Carl Duncan. Especially to Gizmo, Hula and Budweiser (Buddy or Bud for short).

They ran over and greeted him the instant he walked through the door, jumping on him and licking his hands and cheeks. He greeted them right back with hugs and kisses and the same smiley face I had seen in photographs with Penny from their hide-and-seek days. Then he introduced me to all three.

Gizmo was not discriminating about food. He preferred cheese but he also liked nuts and pretzels. He ate anything except what we were served in the mess hall, odd since that tasted like dog food to us.

Budweiser got his name because of his taste for the brew, but he was not partial to any one brand. He slurped up anything alcoholic in his water bowl as long as it had foam.

Hula, the only female in the trio, wagged her tail constantly and got *her* name because she moved her ass in a sexy way (enticing enough to get Gizmo and Bud to abandon food and beverage and come running whenever they spotted her).

Duncan's trio of friends demanded the ritual petting on his arrival and trailed him to the bar, where he ordered dinner and liquid refreshments for them (plus a ginger ale for him and me, producing some minor laughter from other customers).

After their first course was dispensed, another member of the Canine Club joined us. This terrier, named Sergeant, appeared with his best buddy, a human named Roger Rochet (otherwise known to us as Roger Roach).

Roachy was the first air force man I met on The Rock—mostly the services were segregated. I learned that Sergeant and RR found each other a few days after Roachy arrived. And everywhere that RR went, little Sergeant was sure to follow. They stood in the flight line together. After work, Sergeant waited for his pal in front of the mess hall. S. slept under the tent flap by Roger's bunk (the air force men lived in tents). Sergeant also followed him to the beach for the tests. Roachy had goggles (the air force men did) and said he would have put them on Sergeant's head if they had fit. Instead, he held the dog between his legs with one hand over the animal's eyes. Sergeant didn't like it, but RR said that he had to put up with it for only a few seconds.

Roachy and Duncan began an animated conversation about (what else?) the other island dogs. They agreed that a large mutt named Worthless had an IQ problem. He wandered around the island with a few small rocks in his mouth and dropped them only when somebody offered him food. When he was finished eating, he picked up the rocks again and went on his way.

Rider took the bus all the time. When he wanted to get off, he walked to the front and the driver stopped, opened the door and let him out.

And finally Fang, a noisy terrier with a bite worse than his bark, who was taught by some enlisted men to snap at officers. Not surprisingly, Fang vanished from The Rock one day, suddenly and mysteriously. The culprit(s) were never apprehended, although a few of us made a wild guess about their rank(s). From then on, Fang was officially expunged from the canine Who's Who.

Tonight the fleet was in, so, along with Roger Roach, this was an all-service evening. Navy men rarely showed up at the Snakepit, but tonight there were half a dozen. Two of them observed Animal Central and came over. Hands and paws were shaken.

The taller one, a curly-haired redhead named Okie, said, "I joined the navy to see the world. I didn't know they were talking about The Rock!"

"Don't exaggerate," his buddy Norman said. "You've seen Japtan too!" Another island on Eniwetok Atoll.

Okie cackled with laughter and looked at Carl and me. "If you ever get there, be sure and have dinner. The food is terrific."

Norman smiled. "Don't listen to him," he told us. "Okie's only repeating what our ship's security officer told us before we went ashore. That asshole said the fish and fruit made wonderful eating."

Norman told us they spent the afternoon diving off the Japtan pier and then hauled their dinner onto land, fifty-pound clams from the bottom of the lagoon. Before they could eat their chowder, a civilian biologist came over—his Geiger counter clicking like crazy thirty feet from the clams. And just as noisy next to the dessert they had planned, hard-shell bananas. Which turned out to be coconuts that had mutated.

Okie laughed. "We got even when we got back to the ship. We thanked the security officer for his food advice and told him to be sure and eat the giant clams the next time he was on Japtan."

I laughed. So did Duncan but in a hesitant, uncomfortable way.

We were joined by another sailor, who had a flushed face and a bald head. Baldy, as his buddies called him, said that a few hours after Cherokee, he and his shipmates were told it was safe to go ashore on Bikini Island, twenty miles from ground zero. They played softball and drank beer until they noticed their film badges had changed color. They rushed back to the ship at the same instant the whistle and foghorn alerted them to return at once. As soon as everyone was aboard, the ship steamed away from Bikini with all the doors, hatches and ventilation systems closed.

"The next morning my hair started falling out in clumps," Baldy said. "And my gums began to bleed." He grinned, flashing a bloody red smile.

Duncan was holding Hula. He turned pale and put her down on the floor.

A couple of other navy men came over and played "Can You Top This?" They told us they were speeding along after Cherokee when the men on deck were drenched by an unexpected downpour that made the Geiger counters sound like machine guns. The captain knew they had been seriously exposed to radiation and turned on the wash-down system to hose them off.

"Except he didn't use freshwater," one of the sailors explained to us. "He soaked us with ocean water contaminated from the fallout. What he did was expose us to more radiation."

His buddy took over: "Our faces turned bright red and the next day most of us came down with a high fever. I still have one, but the captain said not to worry. It would go away pretty soon." The sailor looked skeptical.

Duncan turned to me and said he was ready to leave, and minutes later we were out the door.

But Okie, who had almost eaten the clams, came running after us.

"Hey, wait a minute," he shouted. "I want to show you something."

It was pitch-black outside the Snakepit when Okie took off his sneakers. "Get a load of this," he said, exposing his bare feet. We looked. And saw his toenails glowing in the dark.

Okie laughed. And so did I. To be polite.

Duncan sprinted off, and I heard him a few hundred yards away. He was retching at the side of the road.

GROUND ZERO IN SHORTS
AND SNEAKERS

———— ⚛ ————

TONY'S PALPITATIONS CONTINUED—HIS HEART RACED, ESPECIALLY IN BED LATE at night. And during the day he was still short of breath for long periods.

"I know it's nothing," he told me. "But maybe I should see a doctor anyway. Just in case." As if I had never suggested that and it was all his own idea.

"No problema," he told me when he returned from his physical. "I'm in good shape."

He said that all three doctors were putting in long hours and seemed like dedicated, conscientious men. Very different from my own experience—which I had never told him about.

"Then why do you look so grim?" I asked.

"Me? There's nothing grim about me."

"You're sure?" I asked.

He was silent. And then: "There were six patients in the hospital. Navy men I talked to. Thirty minutes after one of the tests, they were all sent to check out ground zero. The scientists with them were wearing radsafe clothes."

"And they weren't?"

"They were wearing shorts and sneakers. They didn't even bring T-shirts with them."

"Isn't that against safety regulations?" I asked.

Today I know better. I know that in the 1950s the military was trying to prove that ground zero could be safely occupied soon after an H-bomb blast. They also wanted to learn the effects of radiation on men not wearing protective suits. Many sad mistakes were made, but not all of them were accidents.

Tony told me: "The lieutenant in charge of their unit was wearing shorts and sneakers too. He told them the captain said it was okay, and the scientists always make a big deal about everything."

"So now they're all here in the hospital?"

"Except the lieutenant. He's back in the States. In the hospital. The scientists are fine."

"Naturally. So how are the guys you talked to doing?"

"Lousy. They've got radiation burns. On their chests, arms and legs. The soles of their feet are covered with blisters, and they have rashes all over their bodies. Two of them were puking the whole time I was there, and one guy's hair had turned white. One of them told me that his thighs and waist were once covered with dark lesions. They felt dry and leathery. Eventually they peeled off and left white skin."

"Good God," I said.

"They told me every muscle and bone in their bodies has ached since they went to ground zero, but they weren't complaining. They said it was worth it."

"They did?"

"Yup. It means they're getting out of here. They're going home at the end of the week, and they can't wait."

"No wonder you look upset," I said.

"I'm not upset. That's the army. Shit happens and you have to deal with it. You don't have any choice."

"Where'd you get that from?"

"My old man. He was a career officer."

"He was?"

"Didn't I tell you? He was a big deal. He made it all the way up to bird colonel before he retired." I could tell Tony was impressed—not that he'd ever admit it.

"You never mentioned it."

"He wanted me to go to West Point. He had it all set up with our congressman."

Tony had never mentioned that either. "You didn't get in?"

He shook his head. "Didn't apply. Really pissed the old man off." Tony laughed. "But that's *his* problem. No way am I going to end up a rigid army bastard like he is. And, as for the navy men, you can't let stuff like that get to you."

"It's only a matter of mind over matter."

"That, and self-discipline," he said, not getting it.

A few days later, Tony mentioned Tricia, the girl he had been dating back home before he left for The Rock. It was the first time he had spoken about her in months.

"I've been thinking about her a lot lately."

"What happened to your famous self-discipline?"

"Nothing."

"So write her a letter."

"I'm not going to do that. It would be a sign of weakness."

"It would be a sign that you've been thinking about her."

"That's not how I see it," he said, making it clear that the conversation was over.

That night, half an hour after Lights Out, the bed above mine began to shake and the springs squeaked.

A few minutes later, I heard his low, soft moan.

MAKING THE ISLAND SAFER

Contrary to conventional wisdom, it wasn't better the second time around. Not fallout, anyway. Just as bad but different.

Seminole, Number 6, was one of the most complex tests in Operation Redwing: a surface explosion that simulated an underground explosion. A large tank of water contained a circular chamber ten feet off center, and inside was a 1,832-pound bomb. A box inside a box inside a box.

By the time the fireball reached the wall of the tank, the shot changed from thermal radiation–driven growth to shock wave–driven growth.

By the time the soldiers reached the supply depot, the shock was fallout number two.

Again the D.V. told us to get inside and close the windows, but he seemed calmer today. On-the-job training. With practice, he was becoming a real professional. I was happy for him. Though maybe I shouldn't be so happy for *him.* Perhaps he was broadcasting from inside a lead box (with windows that closed).

Inside the depot, we were quiet. Most of us continued to type, although some men stopped and stared blankly into space in a good imitation of Major Vanish. Captain Weiss looked at requisitions, turning over page after page.

I stopped working and listened to the radiological survey meter. The rain was coming down at a steady rate. The volume and the speed of the clicking never changed. Monotonous sounds that might have lulled me to sleep. If I didn't know what they were.

Suddenly the downpour and the clicking became faster and louder. After a few moments they stopped completely. Seconds later they began again, quicker and noisier than before.

In my (fortunately) brief experience, that wasn't the way fallouts worked. They didn't start and stop and start again that quickly—like our bedsprings. I wondered why today was different. I considered asking someone and getting an opinion, but I didn't bother. What difference would it make?

This time, Estabrook didn't even try to close the windows. At first, I assumed he now accepted what Berko referred to as the old-timer point of view—that it was a waste of time to keep on fighting because no one could ever make anything better on The Rock.

Estabrook remained at his desk. He wasn't typing and he wasn't staring. He was talking. Not to anyone in particular. Maybe to himself. But he was speaking with great passion: "I'm not going to sit here and fry. I'm going to do something about it. Maybe not this minute, but one of these days I'm going to change things around here. I'm not going to sit here and fry. I'm going to do something about it."

Not the words of an old-timer who had given up. Who had become resigned like the rest of us. I had a hunch he *was* going to do something, though apparently not this morning.

Estabrook, the gardener. He told me once that "the woman behind every tree" was a grim joke on him. He already had a woman he loved and he didn't want another. It was the trees and shrubs and bushes he missed. Including the ones in his home and greenhouse.

His wife had written him that the pieces of shell and coral he sent looked beautiful when she put them in the clay pots filled with their plants and flowers—they cheered her up and made her feel he was back with her. A week later she wrote that all the plants and flowers were dead. She took the coral and the shells (wearing asbestos gloves) and buried them all in a deep hole in their backyard.

When he told me that all the plants and flowers had died, I burst out laughing. And couldn't stop. Estabrook looked hurt and angry and I apologized, but even as I was telling him how sorry I was, I still couldn't contain my laughter. All the plants and flowers were dead in one week! How much time did we have left?

I sat in the depot and looked at Estabrook telling us and himself that he was going to do something.

I looked at Straletti. Round-faced and ten pounds overweight when I got to The Rock but drawn and underweight now—and not from the Mrs. Berkowitz Diet. Straletti was part of a big jolly Italian family, and at home there was always plenty of food and wine and celebrating. When he got out of the army, he was going to be a butcher like his dad, and he was looking forward to that. He told me he wouldn't have any trouble dealing with the bomb if he could eat just one good meal.

In the barracks, Straletti was spending afternoons staring at the ceiling. And not at his taped cutouts. No more talks with Marilyn. No more laughing. These days, he had The Kilmer Look, named (by me) after the first man I had seen on The Rock who stared into space for hours at a time. A standard Eniwetok syndrome. Of course, Kilmer had played imaginary musical instruments too. Major Vanish and Jason Underwood exhibited the symptom in a purer form.

At the depot this morning, Straletti stared. And ate biscotti, Italian cookies his mother sent him. Grabbing them from his desk drawer. Once upon a time, he shared them, but he was now hoarding them all for himself. I wondered if they helped him deal with the fallout. I could see they didn't stop him from losing weight.

I watched Richter open up his desk and take out a bottle of mouthwash. He gargled and rinsed and swallowed. He wasn't spitting it out because this wasn't Listerine. It was Jack Daniel's he had sneaked out of the Snakepit. He was going there every afternoon after work and getting so drunk he could barely make it to the barracks on his own. Three days ago, he "pulled a Carl" when he got back—he threw up. On himself and on his bed. And in the middle of his performance, he announced that the mess hall slop looked the same coming up as it did going down. And tasted the same. Then he passed out. The men wrapped him up in his own puke-filled sheet, and when the stink got too bad they threw a bucket of water over him. He didn't wake up.

Today he alternated between mints and Jack Daniel's and then fell asleep at his desk.

While Richter was taking his nap, I thought and remembered. It wasn't my entire life flashing before my eyes. It was my entire week. Highlights of the past seven days.

I thought about the sailors at the Snakepit. The bald man with the bloody gums whose hair had fallen out in clumps. The guys with Fallout Fever. Okie, whose toenails glowed in the dark.

I thought about Carl Duncan. Who used to swim. And wasn't going into the water at all anymore.

I thought about Roger Roach, who said to Duncan he could tell in the shower which men serviced the planes. They had red radiation rings circling their waists. Roachy himself had absorbed thirteen times the MPE (maximum permissible exposure). He had often been scheduled to ship out, but every time he was about to leave, the air force increased the allowable dosage. Roachy remained on duty.

I thought about the pilots flying through mushroom clouds who were told they were not in any danger even though they were exceeding the MPE. And even more than Roachy was.

I thought about Jason Underwood, who said the Devil was with us on The Rock. He told me once during a surface burst that the light rising from the ground was coming from holes in the roof of hell.

I thought about the guy who jumped into the lagoon near the Snakepit and kept shouting that he was going to swim home. Until three men in a boat fished him out of the water three hours later. The Eniwetok Coast Guard?

I thought about "the ear men" Tony told me about. They woke up one morning with their faces literally glued to their pillows. Ears leaking brown goo. They were treated at the dispensary for a fungus and after they rested on beds, the hospital pillows were stained brown.

This linen wasn't laundered but dumped in with the HazMat waste for permanent and immediate disposal.

I thought about the scientist Berko met who worked on Parry, the next island (where there was excellent food). Berko asked him about the two bright stationary lights he and some other men had spotted near the mushroom cloud during Cherokee. The scientist explained they were stars not normally seen from Earth, but the intense heat had burned away the atmosphere around the fireball and made the two stars visible.

I thought about the bulldozer left on Runit by mistake. It melted.

I thought about the men in the hospital with radiation burns and lesions. And I kept telling myself how lucky I was. But why why why didn't that make me feel better?

Mostly I thought about the conversation I'd overheard that morning in the breakfast line. Jason Underwood was in front of me talking to an MP in front of him.

"How do you like being an MP?" Jason Underwood asked.

The MP was round and short and like the sailor at the Snakepit he was bald, but *his* head was shaved.

"It's a big responsibility," the MP replied, with just a touch of arrogance. "We have a lot of important things to do around here."

"Like what?"

The MP had a gravelly voice and lowered it a little, but I could still hear him. "We have to check out all the buildings at night and make sure they're locked up and secure. We have to be certain there aren't men inside doing things they shouldn't be doing—we drive without headlights so no one knows we're coming. We patrol along the ocean and the lagoon and in the barracks during the movies. We walk up and down the beaches. We're on the lookout for troublemakers. We gotta take them by surprise, if you know what I mean."

"I'm not sure I do."

"Faggots." He whispered, but I could still make out his words clearly. "It's our job to get rid of them. They're like Commies. You let your guard down and they take over. We see to it that doesn't happen."

"Ever catch any?" Jason Underwood asked.

"Can't talk about the scorecard. Not allowed. But you can take my word for it—we work hard every day making the island safer."

TWO WAYS TO DEAL WITH
THE BOMB

CARL DUNCAN SEEMED TO BE FEELING BETTER. NOT EXACTLY HAPPY, BUT HE didn't look quite so depressed anymore. Why the improvement? A simple and peculiar explanation. He was now taking long walks.

Back home he wandered through the woods for hours and hours whenever he felt tense and anxious, and after he finished, he was himself again. It worked in Wisconsin, he thought, so why not try it on The Rock?

Carl said to me, half seriously, that maybe it was genetic since his two grandfathers went hiking all the time.

"They sort of brought me up," he told me once, and at first I wondered if his childhood had been as strange as mine. It turned out I had no competition from him in that department, but *his* had definitely been offbeat.

The two men grew up best friends in their small hometown and remained that way all their lives. They married two local women who were twins, and the four of them spent most of their time together. One couple had a son, the other a daughter: They were Carl's mother and father.

Carl loved his parents, but he was closest to his two grandfathers. They were carpenters and (naturally) they were in business together. He called them both "Uncle," and Carl Lester Duncan was named after them. Uncle Carl and Uncle Lester taught him how to swim and fish and whittle wood, and when he was ten, he said, they saved his life. He was fishing in the rapids when he slipped and started to go under, and they ran over to him shouting, "Don't drop the pole!" He realized later they wanted him to concentrate on the fishing pole so he wouldn't panic, and their psychology worked. He trusted them and hung on and they pulled him out.

And now he was following in their footsteps. Literally. Hiking around the island from one end to the other. Walk therapy! A funny solution to his problem on an island as tiny as Eniwetok and a strange way of dealing with atomic fears. But it seemed to work for him and that was all that mattered.

Estabrook was not a walker, but he came up with a way to solve *his* atomic dilemma.

He typed up a requisition for Naval Jelly, a lubricant that could make the windows closable, and he listed the appropriate item name and arms supply catalog number.

"It's a long shot," I said when he showed it to me. "We're not allowed to initiate requisitions on our own."

"I don't care what kind of a shot it is," he said. "I'm submitting it."

I was surprised when the requisition slipped through. I didn't know if the terminally unconscious Major Vanish had stamped the papers APPROVED while he was in his coma. Or if Captain Weiss was responsible and understood exactly what he was doing.

Two hours later Captain Weiss called Estabrook to his desk. "Nice try," he said. "But Major Maxwell wants to see you right away. Good luck."

I watched him leave and crossed my fingers.

When he returned, he told me what happened. The major held the requisition by a single corner. "What is this all about?"

"Naval Jelly is used in boatyards to remove rust and corrosion,"

Estabrook told him. "We can use it to clean up the windows and close them. It will give us some protection during fallouts."

The major shook his head. "Not necessary. We don't have fallouts here."

"But, sir, the radiological survey meter was clicking yesterday morning for three hours."

"We're not going to make liars out of Joint Task Force Seven by putting in a requisition that will permit us to close windows during fallouts that don't exist."

"But we don't have to tell them what the Naval Jelly is *for*," Estabrook suggested.

The major whispered. "They're very smart over there. They'll know what we're up to even if we don't spell it out for them."

"But, sir," Estabrook began.

"Request denied."

"We're being ordered to close the windows. The voice on the loudspeaker—"

"Soldier! You're dismissed!"

After I heard his play-by-play, I said what Captain Weiss had earlier: "Nice try."

"Not so fast. It's not over yet. We'll just have to think of something else."

He refused to be defeated. The least I could do was follow his example. And then it hit me. I thought about the aspirin Nancy was sending me in every letter.

"Ask your wife to send you Naval Jelly from Colorado," I suggested.

He grinned. "That's the answer!"

"The only trouble is, they'll never let us put it on the windows," I said.

"Don't be so negative!" Estabrook told me. "Don't let The Rock do that to you!"

He reminded me I had a key to the office and went there almost every night. "We'll do it in the evening," he said. "You and me. Joint Task Force Two!"

So hope was not gone.

WILSON'S SMILE

WILSON'S BROOM WAS GONE.

He came back from the mess hall, opened up the broom closet and was surprised to see it was empty. He *always* left the broom there, though maybe this one day he had put it somewhere else by mistake. Or maybe somebody else had.

He checked out the room but it wasn't there either. He returned to the closet and opened the door another time—still nothing inside. He went back again and again, and each time he looked, the empty closet squeezed the air out of his chest and forced him to lean forward (a little like Noonen) and to stoop over. Each time, his body sagged and collapsed, and he was years older in seconds.

Confusion took over his face. Where was the broom? He couldn't understand what was happening. What had gone wrong?

He scoured the room. He looked on the floor under his bed. He lifted up his mattress. He rubbed his hand over the blanket to feel for a bulge. He checked the other beds in the room and then the other rooms, all of them, one at a time, over and over. He looked outside the windows and on the roof. Hour after hour. All day and into the night too. A continuous replay of the present and the past. A constant attempt to come to terms with the new reality.

It took days before Wilson finally understood the broom was gone for good. The awareness arrived suddenly. I could see it happening. I could see the abrupt change in his features. The final realization came as an invisible blow. An unseen fist challenging his face, and the pain was right there in front of me flowing along the concrete floor.

Wilson now knew he had not accidentally placed the broom in some corner he shouldn't have. Nobody had borrowed it and put it back in the wrong place by mistake. No one was playing a joke on him. At last he knew for certain it was not going to turn up again in some unexpected spot. The broom, like his routine, was just not there anymore. So how was he going to keep everything clean? The concrete around his bed, the rest of the room, the rest of the barracks, the island, the world?

All of us realized the broom was gone for good. We asked for a new one but we were turned down. Orders from Major Maxwell. MM heard about the man who swept all the time. Said it was bad for morale. Gave the company a bad name. "You have to stop these things before they get out of hand. It's important to follow the rules."

Nobody knew what he meant. But some of the men blamed Billy Byrne. Not that anyone believed BB had spoken to Major Maxwell. But they figured that somehow the mud episode could have brought Wilson to the major's attention.

Right after Billy Byrne led the barracks in the anti-Wilson war, Tony said to me: "You still think Billy Byrne is such a swell kid?"

I didn't have much of an opinion on that particular subject, and I had no intention of falling into a Tony Trap and defending him. I just shut up. But I felt sorry for Wilson. Like Chester who petted the skull, he shouldn't have been on The Rock.

Tony didn't let up on me: "I notice you didn't stop Billy Byrne. You were quick to criticize *me* for encouraging Eder, but you encouraged Billy Byrne. By not speaking up."

He was right. Duncan, at least, walked out. But I hung around and watched and kept my mouth closed. Naturally, Tony didn't say anything either, but that's what Tony was like. More than once he had told me his number one rule on The Rock: Never Get Involved.

I didn't want to be like him. I regretted not protecting Wilson then, but there was nothing I could do about it now.

Two days after the broom disappeared, Wilson turned stiff. He marched around the room briefly, then stood at attention and remained that way. I assumed he was responding to instructions from a voice or voices that I (a mere mortal) could not hear.

Nobody in the barracks commented on what was going on. Nobody noticed. Everyone was too busy. Busy pretending not to notice. The new Wilson made all of us uncomfortable. Many strange things had already happened on our strange island, but we had never seen anything like this. We had watched the sky open up. More than once. Maybe we were now afraid the ground would open up too.

Sunday was the third day Wilson stood at rigid attention. But I sensed there was some other reason that made the day feel so strange.

Was it the sun? It seemed hotter, burning with a blistering heat that seared the skin.

Was it the barracks? More subdued than usual.

I was on my bed watching Wilson and not watching Wilson. I saw him stand and march again. And soon he stopped marching and turned into another Wilson. Relaxed. Without tension.

"He isn't bothered anymore," Hawkins said.

Eder: "He almost looks content, the way he did when he was sweeping."

"He's adjusting," Craig said. "He's going to be okay."

I said nothing. I watched and waited. And so did Tony. Not stretched out in the chair, his regular spot, but standing up. Just looking.

And then Wilson took an M-1 from the rifle rack, held it by the barrel like a broom and swept the stock back and forth against the floor. No one cared, because the rifle was not loaded. Only the MPs had bullets. Wilson had found a new broom and there was no reason to worry.

The men seemed amused, but after a while they ignored him again. Except for Tony, who continued to watch. And me.

THE ONE-YEAR PAID VACATION · 167

Wilson "swept" for a long while that afternoon and stopped late in the day. For an instant he stood motionless. Then he took the weapon in both hands and turned it, this time holding it by the stock with the barrel pointing down.

I turned away for a moment to grab some aspirin, and just then I heard a loud explosion behind me. I spun around. Wilson had pulled the trigger, but instead of the click of an empty barrel, there was a single crazy blast, a sudden roar, harsh and violent, and someone fell. I saw Tony (aka Kevin Tonnello) collapse onto the concrete and become part of it. He was lying on the floor with his right hand pressing against his right side, red fingers on a brown aloha shirt and the clash of colors sounded like a groan.

Screams and movement, men rushing to the left and right and diving under beds, dashing into the hallway and Don't Be Next! Trying to turn themselves into Supermen and run faster than speeding bullets. Shouting *Stop it!* as if words were going to change anything now.

I ran toward Wilson. I wanted to grab his rifle and keep him from shooting again at Tony or anyone else (including me) but I didn't have to hurry. He did not fight or flee or try to fire a second bullet. He put the rifle down. Laid it on his bed and sat on the floor and waited. Waited for something to happen. Waited for someone to come.

The second thing I did (sorry Tony, it wasn't the first) was make sure the medics were on the way. Tony was still alive right now this minute and I wanted him to stay that way.

I told Estabrook to get to the hospital fast. But he said Duncan had sprinted there as soon as Wilson pulled the trigger.

Tony was not running. He was lying on the floor with his left arm over his face. Maybe shielding himself from the image of Wilson aiming the rifle at him a second time and shooting again. Emptying out whatever life still remained in him.

His eyes were shut. And so were his lips. He was not looking and not talking. Not answering my questions: "How are you? What can I do?"

Not moving. Curled on the floor with a pulse but how far away from here was dead? Nobody (including Tony) knew how hurt he was, but (to my untrained eyes) he exhibited few signs of life, so please someone do something to help and hurry. Seconds later (or maybe sooner), the medics carried him off to a hospital that was waiting for him, and I did not find out how he was or if he was until later.

Everyone said poor Tony, poor guy, he didn't deserve anything like that, but underneath their sympathetic expressions: Relief. Thank God it wasn't me. Promise not to tell anyone but it was sort of fun (as long as it wasn't me bleeding on the floor) and I almost enjoyed myself. A bullet piercing the monotony.

"I was watching Wilson before Tony jumped him," Eder said. "He was aiming the rifle at Billy Byrne."

"I saw it too," Hawkins said. "Too bad Wilson didn't shoot the man he was aiming at." He looked around to see Billy Byrne's expression and seemed disappointed that he wasn't in the room.

"Billy Byrne asked for it," Noonen said. "It was all his fault." Several heads nodded up and down.

"We'll get even with *him* one of these days," Hawkins said. Noonen and Eder agreed.

The MPs arrived and took Wilson to the jail. One of the guards put a broom in the cell but it stayed right there against the wall and Wilson never touched it, never even looked at it.

The next morning Wilson was escorted to the airstrip by six MPs, all carrying loaded pistols in their holsters. Not necessary. He was docile. Made no trouble. Did what was asked of him. Weapons not needed with this calm and compliant soldier.

A bunch of us went to the airstrip when he left, and he wasn't staring anymore. His eyes weren't glazed. He looked around but not at the men seeing him off. He looked at the sky and the water and the ground and the buildings and there was a peaceful expression on his face.

In the Some Things Never Change Department, some of the men yelled at him, though for once they were yelling at a departee and not an arrival. And what they yelled (together, in unison, a single multicolored, aloha shirt–wearing animal), what they yelled was: *Hey, Wilson, why don't you sweep The Rock into the ocean?*

And as you might guess, he didn't answer. But he did smile.

So who says Wilson didn't have a sense of humor?

HOW TO EMPTY A HOSPITAL
IN ONE EASY LESSON

—————————— ⚛ ——————————

Tony was back at the Statler two days after Wilson shot him and he was even quieter than usual. It was only after the barracks cleared out at dinnertime and he and I were by ourselves that he began to talk.

He was in the chair, his favorite place, right leg crossed over his left, right foot bouncing up and down. Something he did often. Though at other times he remained perfectly still, as if he were posing for a photograph. No connection I could figure out between leg movement and the coffee crystals he ate all day.

He told me he woke up in the hospital with a piercing headache that sounded like the ones I used to get. That and the bandages on his thigh and lower abdomen made him think he was seriously hurt. A concussion? Internal injuries? But no. The medic assured him the wound was superficial.

"Wilson shoved me away when I lunged for the rifle," he said. "The bullet only grazed me but I fell and landed on the cement floor, back of the head first. A good way to crack your skull. I'm lucky I was only knocked out cold and got a headache."

"How come you tried to grab Wilson's rifle?" I asked. "You. Kevin Tonnello. The man who never gets involved."

He shrugged. "I didn't think about it. I just did it. Instinct, I guess."

"The instinct of a colonel's son?"

Another of his rare (and unrevealing) smiles. And then an explanation: "Something about the way Wilson held his rifle bothered me, and when he fingered the trigger, I was pretty sure there was going to be trouble. I didn't want anyone to get hurt."

"So you got hurt yourself."

His mouth turned up slightly in a half grin. "Serves me right for breaking my own rule."

"He was aiming at Billy Byrne?" I asked.

Tony nodded. "Getting even for the mud, I suppose. Or maybe he blamed the missing broom on Billy Byrne."

"Maybe. But how the hell did Wilson get a bullet?"

"I was thinking about that in the hospital. He probably liberated it from MP headquarters."

"Where they're supposed to keep the ammo locked up."

Tony shrugged. "Guess they're sloppy about it sometimes."

"Obviously Wilson found a way," I said. "So how *was* the hospital? See your old buddies?"

"Just Clem. The rest of them were gone. Three of the sailors were back on the ship."

"Including the guy who said it was worth it because they were going home at the end of the week?"

"You mean Drexel? Yeah. They sent him back too."

"At least he's well enough to be back on duty," I replied, trying to see a bright side.

Tony shook his head. "They were puking less when they left, but they were still running fevers and their skin lesions hadn't cleared up. Clem has them too, on the soles of his feet, and his are so bad he can barely stand. Still, they told him he'll be back on the ship in a day or two if he can walk okay."

"So he can swab the deck on crutches?"

Tony was not in the mood for my grim humor and went on as if I hadn't spoken. "What really got to Clem were the fucking speeches. He told me they had to listen to a lot of crap from the officers when they came to pick up those three guys. About the great job they've done. How proud the navy is. How well they've served their country."

"Sounds like Major Maxwell was the speechwriter," I said. Still no laughs from my audience of one. "What happened to the other two guys?"

"Rosario's in bad shape. He's in a hospital in California."

"And the other guy?"

"Geezer. He's gone."

"Where did he go?"

Tony's features went pale beneath his tan, and for a moment he didn't answer. "They took him away in a body bag," he said finally.

"Jesus Christ!" I replied, stunned.

"Jesus Christ is right. Clem is bitter as hell. He kept saying to me: This is how to empty a hospital in one easy lesson. You stuff one man in a body bag. The other guys are filling up beds, so you send them back on duty. The empty building proves you cured them all."

Tony shut his eyes and pressed the tips of his fingers against his forehead. Trying to push away the memories? Drive out the thoughts that went with them? He reached for his Kiwi and began polishing his shoes.

"He's pissed and I don't blame him. Clem was doing his duty and suddenly all this shit happens, and he has no idea what for. He can't figure out what America is getting out of it," Tony said as he buffed and polished. He looked up for a moment. "Doing stuff like this makes me feel better," he explained. "You know. Keeping busy—"

"I guess it's better than crying," I replied. Tony moved around restlessly in his chair and his eyes darted toward the door. He looked like a man who wanted to run away—but there was nowhere to run to.

We were both silent as he moved the rag back and forth. After a while Tony spoke again. "You go through what happened to these guys and you lose your perspective. I feel bad for Clem. And the others too." He put down the doeskin rag and reached for a nylon stocking. "Makes the final shine brighter," he said as he started moving the stocking back and forth along the heel of each shoe.

"I can also see the other point of view," he went on. "There's a job that has to be done, and it's tough on the officers. They've got hard calls to make. It's *never* easy, but it must be really rough on them now. In the middle of the fucking H-bomb tests. My old man—" He cut himself off, stopped polishing, admired the shine. "I feel much better now. I'm not going to let this shit get to me."

His tone told me that the conversation was over. He tried to stand, but as he got up he staggered and almost lost his balance. As he put out his arm to steady himself, I could see that his hands were shaking.

In the next few days, Tony mentioned the sailors again several times, but whenever he did, he made a point of telling me that he wasn't going to let the conversation with Clem get to him. From the way he looked and spoke, I had no reason to doubt him—he seemed just like the old Tony again. Slightly aloof. Somewhat remote. Faintly detached. But above all, composed and in control.

And yet he was screaming in his sleep. "Some dickhead said this is no shithole," I heard him shout in the middle of the night. "Get me out of here!"

Angry, tortured sounds coming from somewhere deep inside. From a man who was not going to let anything get to him.

Three days later, Tony got a letter from Dr. Tankeray, on the staff of Mount Sinai, Irene's hospital. He wrote that some months earlier Irene had detected lumps in both breasts, but her work schedule was heavy—six days a week with hours a day overtime—and she put off having an examination. When she got around to it, the tumors were well advanced and the biopsies indicated they were malignant. She underwent surgery the next day and was now getting chemotherapy. The doctor was hopeful she would make a full recovery, but that was by no means a certainty. She was currently listed in serious condition.

"I have to be with her," is all that Tony said to me.

He spoke to Captain Wiggs, the officer in charge of his unit at Headquarters Company, and applied for a two-week compassionate leave. He brought along the letter from Dr. Tankeray.

"No dice," Tony told me when he came back. "Wiggs said she's not a close enough relative. It would be different if it were my father or mother, but she's only my father's sister."

"*Only* your aunt?" I said. "There's no one in the world you're closer to."

"Wiggs said that wasn't the only reason he had to turn me down. She's in *serious* condition. She's not *critical*. I told him if she were in critical condition, she'd probably be dead by the time I got home. But he said he was just trying to explain the rules, and with *my* family background, I should know them better than anyone."

"So much for compassion," I said. "What about your bullet wound? Doesn't that count for anything?"

"Not according to Wiggs. He made a big deal about this being a security post. He said they couldn't let me go because we're in the middle of the H-bomb tests."

"As if you hadn't noticed," I said.

"He told me they need me here."

"To type?"

Tony scowled. "According to Wiggs, I'm doing essential work."

"Like the dozens of other typists at Headquarters Company. Couldn't they fill in for you when you're gone?"

"Wiggs wouldn't budge. I even reminded him that my year will be up in a few weeks."

"So you'll be leaving in the middle of the tests anyway."

"Yes, but Wiggs said that's completely different."

"It is? But I'll bet he's grateful for the way you served your country."

Tony didn't respond.

"They sent *you* back to the ship too," I said.

Tony bristled. "I wouldn't put it that way. I can see his point of view too. He's doing his job and following the rules. I only wish the rules didn't apply to me. Anyway, I shouldn't have let the letter get to me. By the time I'm home, Irene will be feeling much better and I'll have a lot more than two weeks to cheer her up."

Typical of Tony. Upbeat and positive no matter what. Determined to believe everything is going to turn out okay. I used to laugh at that side of him, but suddenly I was seeing Tony in a different way.

Sometimes it's hard not to admire a man who refuses to be defeated.

PART FIVE

Mutations

THE THREE HORSEMEN

———— ⚛ ————

THE THREE HORSEMEN OF THE NUCLEAR APOCALYPSE—THAT WAS THE WAY I thought of Hawkins and Noonen and Eder when I was on The Rock. Three men who dealt with their own atomic terrors by terrorizing.

By the time the tests were well under way, they had become buddies and turned into a strange trio. All three of them had changed, and they were changing more and more every day.

I looked at Hawkins's face and I could swear his slitty, squinty eyes were closer together than before. No question anymore that he had the inbred look of the mountain country. And the razor blade never seemed to leave his hand. There were more gashes on his legs, and they were deeper and drew more blood.

Craig said Hawkins got into a fight with Straletti when the three of them were on KP, and Hawkins cut Straletti's arm. "Tell anyone and I'll slit your throat," Hawkins warned. Straletti swore it wasn't true. And the bandage on his arm? He cut himself in the kitchen.

I listened to Hawkins talk about women and what he was going to do to them when he got back home. Force himself inside, and the more they fought back, the better it was going to be. He wanted to shove himself into their cunts. He wanted to watch them bleed. He wanted the sheets stained red, and not because they were having their periods.

And as for Noonen, his wild eyes were bulging. Bright and shiny and sometimes I thought they were going to pop out of his head. He still talked mostly about his wife's new neighbor, the one who was fucking her. He said the guy had moved in with his wife. She didn't exactly write and tell him that, but he could read between the lines, and when he got back to the States, he was going to do something about it. He was not going to let the bastard get away with that kind of shit.

"So what are you going to do?" Berko asked.

"I'm going to cut his fucking nuts off."

"Sounds like a good idea," Berko replied.

"You think I'm kidding? Well, I'm not. I'm fucking serious!"

And none of us doubted it.

Hawkins and Noonen were the same as they were when they arrived only more so. Eder seemed to be another person. He rarely did push-ups and sit-ups anymore, and the good-natured grin was gone for good. He was perpetually moody. Nobody dared to tease him about his girlfriends these days. They didn't want to be on the receiving end of a flashing temper that erupted all too often.

Noonen and Eder developed a strange bond. They talked for hours about their fathers, especially the times their fathers beat them up. They discussed their own childhood "crimes," the ones that provoked paternal fists and those that only merited hard slaps with the palm of the hand.

But differences between them emerged too. Eder's father did more damage: broken arms and cheekbones. For Eder, the best part of his life was Payback Time, when he grew big enough and strong enough to get even. Eder's smile reappeared when he talked about breaking his old man's nose.

Noonen was small and definitely smaller than his father. He was built more like his mother, he said. He was never able to enjoy the pleasures of retribution but, unlike Eder, he admired his dad's skills as a fighter.

"You should have seen the way he beat the shit out of my mother," Noonen said, exploding with laughter, eyes wilder than ever.

Eder: "My dad did that too, but I never found it funny." He looked grim and sad. "I loved my mother. I still do. It ripped me up when that son of a bitch punched her and made her bloody—before I got big enough to stop him."

Eder was crying at night these days, softly, trying to conceal the sounds from the other men. The expression I imagined on his face when he was sobbing in the dark was the same look I saw when he talked about his battered mother.

Hawkins and Noonen and Eder went to the airstrip every afternoon to yell "White Meat" at the newcomers. I thought about the three men I had stared at when I got off the plane, drool sliding out the side of at least one mouth. I remembered their expressions. Cruel. Crazy. Pathetic. And I suspected that the faces of Hawkins, Noonen and Eder looked that way now when *they* were at the airport.

I remembered Berko's question of months ago: Does the island change the men, or is this how they are when they arrive? My silent answer at the time was both. Now I considered another possibility. Maybe Atomic Island changes them. Tests began at the Pacific Proving Ground in 1946 and radiation has been there ever since.

Maybe Hawkins and Noonen and Eder had mutated into a new species, the same one as the trio that greeted me when I arrived.

Human versions of the banana-shaped coconuts and the three-eyed fish.

A BIG PAIR OF TITS

"I WISH I COULD GET LAID RIGHT NOW," EDER ANNOUNCED TO ALL OF US.

Eder had changed, but his favorite sentence remained the same. And soon after Wilson left The Rock, Hawkins came up with a reply: "There's always Billy Byrne."

Noonen stared when Billy Byrne took off his shirt. "I'll never forget what a good pair of tits are like when he's around."

The men in our room looked over and so did the guys from the other rooms, hanging out in ours as usual.

Billy Byrne had tits like a woman. He walked to his footlocker, and the layers of fat that covered his entire body rolled around and bounced up and down with every step. He bent over for his towel and the fat on his chest dangled down.

"Man, he's really stacked," Hawkins said.

"I could sure use a broad right now," Eder announced.

"I'd love a handful of tit," Hawkins said. "From *her*."

Billy Byrne ignored them. He took an aloha shirt from his footlocker and faced away as he put on the shirt, but he didn't button it. When he turned around, it hung open but covered his chest.

"What's the matter with you?" Hawkins asked. His razor blade was in his left hand. "The only good pair we've seen close up and you want to hide them?"

"You're not funny," Billy Byrne said, even as some of the men laughed.

"I think he's hilarious, and so does everyone else," Eder told Billy Byrne, bending his elbow to make his biceps look larger. And more threatening. "Now open up and give us a good look."

Billy Byrne walked to the door. "I'm going to take a shower," he announced in a pouty voice. He had a towel in his right hand.

Hawkins stretched out a leg and blocked his path. "You're not going anywhere. We're not finished with you yet."

"Let me go!" Billy Byrne squealed. It came out as a question.

"Maybe. But don't be in such a hurry," Noonen said.

Billy Byrne tried to climb over Hawkins's leg but Hawkins raised it. Billy Byrne stopped, looked around the room and saw all eyes focused on him. He turned back to the door, arms at his side, and waited for Hawkins to move his leg. Instead, Hawkins reached out and grabbed the towel.

"Come on!" Billy Byrne whined. "Let me have it."

" 'Let me have it,' " Hawkins mimicked. "We'll let you have it, all right."

Then he folded the towel and snapped it at Billy Byrne's stomach.

Billy Byrne recoiled from the sting and touched the red spot left by the towel. "Owwwww."

Hawkins laughed. "What will you give me if I let you have your precious towel?"

Billy Byrne shrugged his shoulders.

"You know what you're going to give us? A little feel, that's what," Hawkins said. Then he turned to some of the men from down the hall, gathering near our door to see what was going on. "Look at those boobs! Don't they make you feel horny as hell?"

The men nodded. "Oh, yeah! Billy Byrne's got a great pair!" someone said and everybody agreed.

Billy Byrne attempted to climb over the leg again, but Hawkins wouldn't let him pass. Billy Byrne tried to be casual and he crossed his arms in front. The gesture squeezed the fat together and made his breasts look larger.

"Way to go, Babe," Noonen said. "You're better than anything I've seen in ages."

"You want your towel?" Hawkins told Billy Byrne. "Then pick it up." He held the towel above Billy Byrne's head and let it fall to the floor.

Billy Byrne squatted down, but before he could grab it, Eder snatched the towel away.

"No squatting," Eder said, announcing the rules. "Bend down for it."

Billy Byrne straightened up and the towel went to the floor once more. "Bend over and you can keep it," Eder said.

Billy Byrne decided to try again. He leaned over the way Eder told him and his flab dropped down.

"Beautiful! That's what we want to see," Noonen said.

Just as Billy Byrne touched the towel, Hawkins moved forward, gently cupping his right hand under a dangling breast. Billy Byrne jerked away with the towel in his hand.

"Great, truly superb, and I've felt the best of them," Hawkins declared with a glow of accomplishment. He nodded to the other men. Bowing slightly. As if acknowledging applause.

Billy Byrne walked to the bed and buttoned his shirt.

"You could really clean up here if you decide to be nice to us—" Eder said.

And then Noonen shouted: "We want a feel too!"

The men at the door laughed again and nodded their heads, but Billy Byrne turned his back. He took a toothbrush and toothpaste from his shelf and walked toward the door. Hawkins stepped in front of him, blocking his way.

Billy Byrne tried to push his way through, but Hawkins stood firm. "Simon says you don't have permission to go," he told Billy Byrne.

Billy Byrne's eyes darted around the cement floor: "I . . . I . . . I . . . just want to brush my teeth," he said.

"We know what you just want to do," Noonen told him, "but not right now. We want a little feel first."

Billy Byrne backed up. Hesitant and uncertain. He put his tooth-brush and toothpaste on the bed and picked up a copy of *Life* maga-zine. He continued to stand as he thumbed through the pages, trying to look nonchalant.

Hawkins, still in front of him, cleaned his fingernails with his razor blade. His head was down and he seemed to be concentrating on his hands, but his eyes followed all of Billy Byrne's movements.

"What are you reading, Billy Byrne?" Noonen asked.

"Looking at a magazine. I'm not bothering you. Go away," Billy Byrne answered, his voice cracking.

Noonen brought his palm down straight on the magazine and knocked it to the floor.

"Reading isn't on your schedule now," Eder said. "You're about to make some men happy." He reached out, and Billy Byrne brushed the arm away.

"You looking for a fight, Billy Byrne?" Hawkins wanted to know.

"I'm lookin' for nothin'," was the answer. "Leave me be."

Hawkins backed Billy Byrne up against the window and stretched out his hand again.

Billy Byrne kicked his foot and jabbed Hawkins in the shin. Hawkins lashed out with a fist straight into Billy Byrne's gut. A smile of pleasure took over Hawkins's face.

Billy Byrne bent over in pain, his hand over his stomach. He cov-ered his face and moaned. Half to himself and half as a plea: "Please stop."

Hawkins clapped his hands and laughed. "The little boy can't take it," he said. "Imagine that! He can dish it out but he can't take it. I think he'll behave now."

Hawkins stopped laughing and turned to Noonen. "You want a feel too, right?" he said. "He'll be happy to oblige."

Noonen thrust out his hand toward Billy Byrne and pulled it back quickly. Close but not quite touching. Teasing. Then he stretched out his arm slowly and grabbed the flesh tightly in his fingers. Billy Byrne tried to pry the hand loose. It was futile. Finally Billy Byrne raised up his knee into Noonen's stomach. The blow caught him off guard, and Noonen let go and backed off in surprise.

"Hawkins is right. It's a nice big soft squooshy boob. 38D, I'll bet,"

Noonen announced, licking his lips. Everyone laughed. Noonen's features hardened and then he wheeled around to face Billy Byrne. "I don't like being kicked in the stomach. No one messes with me like that and gets away with it. You need a lesson."

Billy Byrne put up his arms to protect himself but Noonen took hold of a wrist in both hands and twisted in opposite directions. An Indian burn.

"Say you're sorry," Noonen told Billy Byrne.

A low groan of pain.

"I didn't hear 'Sorry,' " Noonen said, twisting harder.

Billy Byrne didn't answer. "Owww," he moaned, and Noonen released his wrist.

"All we want is a few good feels, just like you got," Eder said to Noonen. "I didn't get anything like that. You think he's got something against me?" And then Eder turned to Billy Byrne: "You're showing favorites. Nobody likes that. We all want a piece of titty, just the same as Noonen and Hawkins."

The men at the door murmured *Yes* and electricity invaded the room. Billy Byrne started to run but Hawkins shouted "Grab him!" and Noonen did. He took an arm and forced it behind Billy Byrne's back. "Now hold still while Eder gets a real feel," Hawkins said.

Eder placed his palm an inch from Billy Byrne's chest and held it there. He moved it from side to side close to the shirt without touching it. Billy Byrne followed the fingers with his eyes but did not move. Then he reached out with his free hand to strike his tormentor. A feeble slap that grazed Eder's shoulder.

Eder laughed and shook his head.

"Getting violent, are you?" Hawkins said. He turned to Noonen, who was still holding Billy Byrne. "Teach him how to behave."

Noonen pulled the arm up behind Billy Byrne's back until he fell to his knees in pain and fought to hold back tears. After a moment, Noonen eased his grip and Billy Byrne relaxed but did not move. He knew that any resistance would bring back the pain.

Billy Byrne looked up sadly. He was at their mercy.

"I don't want you to do it," Billy Byrne said, whining now, begging. "Please leave me alone."

But they didn't. He was trapped. Caught. Cornered and tears in his eyes at the twist of an arm. He had no chance.

Hawkins put his fingers under the aloha shirt and squeezed. Billy Byrne lashed out again with his free hand but missed his target.

"Open his shirt," Eder said. "It's no fun unless we can see those boobs."

Noonen opened the shirt and it was time now for everyone to have fun. Austin, from across the hall, touched Billy Byrne. "Man, they're wonderful," he said. Closed eyes and pleasure on his face.

"You go next," Hawkins said to Petrakis.

Petrakis moved forward. A bounce in his step. Features sparkling with anticipation. Two palms moved around Billy Byrne's boobs. "Boy, it's great to cop a feel," he said.

"Okay, everyone line up," Hawkins ordered. "This is the army. We need a little organization around here."

They stood in single file and waited patiently.

Holt touched Billy Byrne's chest quickly and moved on. "Yeah, that was good."

Winkhauser grabbed the right tit and Billy Byrne made one more attempt to break loose. He tried to shake off his tormentors, but they were holding him too tight. He struck out with his feet but no one was there and all he kicked was air.

"Don't try that again," Hawkins warned. He held Billy Byrne himself and pinched the flab on his upper arm until Billy Byrne yelped. Hawkins apologized to everyone for the interruption: "He'll be more cooperative now."

The noise attracted a dozen more men. They watched from the doorway and took their places at the end of the line. Each one waited for his turn.

Billy Byrne stopped fighting. He stood limp and loose, but the men held him up. He was an inanimate object now.

A BILLION-TO-ONE ODDS

THREE LETTERS FROM NANCY AT MAIL CALL. I KEPT THEM IN MY BACK POCKET UN-opened as usual. I saved them. I savored them. I spent the rest of the afternoon looking forward to them. I knew that after I unlocked the front door of the depot after dinner, I would go to my desk, take Nancy's picture from my locked drawer and prop it against my stapler so I could look at her while I read what she had to say. Then I would light up a Kool cigarette, inhale, exhale, put the pack and the matches on my desk so I would be ready for more cigarettes as I reread her letters for the second and third time (and maybe more).

With my letters—count 'em, folks, three—I walked to the office at a brisker pace than I did on a no-letter (or even a one-letter) evening. As I approached the Snakepit, I saw Carl Duncan sitting on the side of Lagoon Road.

Carl, I knew, had read *his* letters hours before sitting by himself near the lagoon. He was probably about to visit Bud, Hula and Gizmo now. I could see letters (from Penny, I assumed) sticking out of the back pocket of his shorts. I smiled. Two men focused on their girl-friends.

I said hello when I reached him, but he turned away and didn't re-spond. I figured he didn't hear me and spoke again. This time he an-swered. He told me he wanted to be by himself. Understandable (for whatever reason) and not so surprising on The Rock. Except that he sounded almost nasty. Not at all like Carl.

Then he turned toward me. Crying. It wasn't hard for me to figure out why. I had absolutely no intention of leaving him alone (as he had requested) and I told him so.

I asked a few questions, and his sobbing and his silence came to an end. Finally Carl Duncan's words (instead of tears) flooded Lagoon Road.

Penny had met someone new. Those were the exact words in her letter: "I've met someone new." Although the guy really *wasn't* some-one new. Seldom is, I thought. Maybe in New York but not, I figured, in the small Wisconsin town where Carl grew up. This time it was the usual culprit. Carl's best friend. They were both on the high school football team. Carl was the quarterback and Keith, the captain, his best wide receiver.

If we had been in any other place on the globe, I would probably have put my arm around his shoulder as I tried to comfort him. But men on The Rock didn't touch each other, and in that respect I fol-lowed the rules. Instead of hands and arms, I used the only other method available to me to try to make him feel better. I threw a lot of words at him.

I told Carl it was very possible that in a few days or weeks, Penny would come to her senses. And maybe Keith would too.

I told him that someday, after he got off the island, *he'd* meet someone new.

I said: I know it must feel like the end of the world (what a strange phrase to use on The Rock), but things will get better. Believe me. I promise you.

My pompous voice of experience (I had just turned twenty-three) trying to soothe an innocent eighteen-year-old kid (or was he nine-teen now?).

I began a lot of sentences by saying, "I know you won't believe me but . . ." And I was right. I was all over the place in my futile attempt to comfort him. Well-meaning but basically ineffective.

On the other hand, what words *could* I have used to make him feel better? None. At least I *did* communicate my concern and let him know I cared about him. Some men on Eniwetok never did that, especially in the middle of the test series. So, on second thought, maybe I deserved a passing grade.

By the time I left him, Carl's eyes were dry, and I continued down Lagoon Road. But I turned around suddenly and (to my disappointment) I observed him rise to his feet and enter the Snakepit. I realized then (I can be a little slow sometimes) that he had been inside before and that when we spoke, Carl the teetotaler was a little high. Now he was going inside to get a lot high.

I thought: Drinking is not going to help, but I guess you have to find that out for yourself. (Me the wise father to Carl's wayward son.)

But as it turned out, I was the innocent that evening (fittingly). I took Carl at his word. I never imagined he was telling me only part of the truth.

The odds must have been a billion to one that five days later Nancy would write me and use the same phrase Penny did: "I've met someone new." Or maybe not. Maybe that was the standard sentence in every Dear John letter.

Part of me was slightly smug when I had talked to Carl outside the Snakepit: I feel sorry for you, but it's a relief to know it could never happen to me.

The way Major Maxwell once described fallouts: "It can't happen—and certainly not here."

To be absolutely fair to my jilter (and fifty years later that's easy to do), there were two letters involved here: the one I thought I got and the one I *really* got.

Nancy did in fact write me that she had met someone new (happily, not my best friend). He wanted to marry her and she wanted to marry him. IF. If I wasn't going to marry her.

It was blackmail. A gun to my head and I resented it. I especially resented the way she told me. In the middle of a few breezy paragraphs about what life in her hometown of Chicago was like, she wrote me: "Oh, by the way . . ." If I'm exaggerating, it's not by much.

The truth is that she wasn't ditching me for another man (who ironically had the same name as a famous movie star). She was giving me my chance to capture the brass ring. And hand out the gold one.

But I chose not to see it that way. I felt like I was being jilted. And betrayed. She was the only woman in my life in a place where a woman was more important than anywhere else in the world. She was the one person in my life who had helped me get through the rough times on The Rock. Without her, I didn't know how I was going to get through them in the future.

To be absolutely honest (and that's easy too after fifty years), I would never have married Nancy (although I didn't know that in June 1956). I *did* love her, and our days and nights together were fun and sexy and more. But like many other young people, I didn't realize then that love could be much more than what we had. One day (in 1970) I would find out.

Or maybe I did realize it then. I could have written her back: Please please please marry *me*, and she would have. And, in my opinion, we would have lived unhappily ever after.

Instead I told myself (when I was finally able to think again) that my life had just started and I wasn't ready to get married. And more important, I didn't want to make life-altering decisions while I was still on Atomic Island. For many reasons. Not the least of which was that I couldn't be objective—at a place and a time when my need for her was so desperate.

I sent her an answer. I never ended any of my letters to her with the usual "Love" comma. Instead I wrote "Now and Forever." This time I finished up with: "Now and Yesterday." Wow! I was really giving it to her!

And then I made a little bonfire for myself right there at my desk in the depot. I took her picture (leaning against the stapler) and her letter and all her previous letters and a copy of the poem I had written saying that without her I would be "one more grain on a lonely beach." And I made a neat pile. And then I reached for the pack of matches (sitting on top of my Kool cigarettes), which had been waiting eagerly to take part in this important event. And I grabbed the one lucky match and lit it and burned up my past. And I held on to the match long enough to burn my fingers too. Seriously burned, I imagined at the time. Take THAT, Nancy.

But I barely ended up with a blister.

I was not sad or angry or upset. Oh, no. All I wanted was an H-bomb to blow up the whole fucking island with me on it, but the one thing wrong with that particular fantasy was that Nancy would not be there to share it with me.

So what did I have to look forward to now? More fallout. As if there hadn't been fallout enough that evening inside the depot.

And more explosions. Exactly what I was going to get the very next morning, although I didn't know it yet.

In fact, twice the usual number. And at exactly the same hour and minute: 6:26 A.M.

"BY THE WORLD FORGOT"*

THE PREDAWN WAKE-UP CALL. WE MARCHED TO THE LAGOON, STOOD AT ATTEN-tion and waited. For Blackfoot, a two-hundred-foot-high tower shot on poor old Runit (Yvonne), Eniwetok Atoll. And for Flathead—ground zero was the Bikini Atoll lagoon.

We referred to the two of them together as Blackhead (although Flatfoot would have done the job just as well). Today they were coming at us from all sides.

And on all sides I was surrounded by men. Yet I felt completely alone, the way I did every other morning I saw and heard and felt an H-bomb explode. More alone than at any other time in my life. Before and since.

At first I thought I was the only one. Eventually I learned it was not just me.

You feel small. You look up at pieces of the sky in the shape of a

*From the poem "Eloisa to Abelard" by Alexander Pope

mushroom cloud and watch them cover up the sun, stretching out to the ends of horizons and then reaching beyond. You are standing still, but the world around you is speeding up and at the same time moving in slow motion. Both at once. And slowly and quickly you get smaller. And disappear. You cannot find yourself anymore.

That was how it was during every test, and I knew that was how it was going to be this morning.

Four, three, two, one, zero. Once again I am smothered by loneliness. And surrounded not just by one but two devices. I know more than ever now how insignificant and unimportant I am.

Memories return. Images from the past that I do not want to think about. Moments I have erased from my mind so they cannot hurt me anymore, but at this moment I am no longer able to keep them away. The two bombs overpower me, and I am pushed back in time. It is 1948. I am by myself. I am fifteen and I have been left to my own devices.

For years, Fraulein locked the bathroom door with the two of us inside to keep out the outside world. Not that anyone ever tried to turn the knob and enter. But when I was fifteen, I locked the door to keep Fraulein out. And I locked other doors too. I no longer told her everything I did during the day—like so many teenagers, I wanted to keep a part of my life to myself. But Fraulein believed I was taking me away from her.

The answer for her was more codeine. And creating her own imaginary family—she and I were the parents and Frenchy, our wire-haired fox terrier, was our child. She told me Frenchy loved *her* more than me and was always proving it. Whenever she saw me with the dog, she called out (food in hand) and Frenchy trotted over to her. Fraulein gave me a triumphant "I told you so" look and soon played the same game again. Showing *she* was the parent Frenchy cared about.

During that year, Fraulein cried most of the time, just as my father had done in the years after my mother's death. Fraulein's tears were for the death of the child she had raised from birth.

Fraulein could barely function but, despite the advice of relatives, my father wanted her to stay with us—he was grateful to her for filling in as a parent for so long.

Her migraine headaches and her codeine addiction became

worse. I didn't need someone to take care of me but Fraulein did. She was groggy and stoned and incoherent much of the day. My father arranged for a full-time nurse to look after her.

That year, Fraulein had electric shock treatments in our apartment. Many of them. I imagined a long, long black thread covered with pain that made its way through her nerves and arteries.

I heard the screaming when the current raced through her body. And I covered my ears to silence the noise, the way some men did in the depot to drive away the sound of the clicking. I pressed the palms of my hands harder and harder against my face, but her cries were not just inside the apartment, they were inside my head, and when I tried to force them away, they became louder.

After each session she wandered through the rooms much more dazed than she used to be under codeine. She asked: "Where's Michael? Where's Michael?" She asked Frenchy. She asked the furniture. She asked me.

Her words reminded me of the question I had asked over and over after my mother died. I wandered around the apartment then and said to everyone: "Where's Mommy? Where's Mommy?" I have no memory of that and no memories of my mother. But relatives told me it happened, and for most of my adult life, tears took over my eyes whenever I thought about the child who said, "Where's Mommy?" Somehow my body and my tear ducts remembered what I could not. And returned me to the sad days when I had just learned how to speak. But not how to understand.

"Where's Michael? Where's Michael?" I was fifteen and I didn't know anymore. I was angry at Fraulein and sorry for Fraulein and, worst of all, sorry for myself.

The H-bomb had the power to make me remember chunks of my childhood I had forced myself to forget. A space voyage back in time that compelled me to stare again at the empty years. Wasn't I better off with my eyes closed?

Thirty seconds after zero hour, I was given permission to open up my eyes.

I watched Blackfoot's anvil-headed cloud soar to a height of 32,000 feet, 10,000 more than expected, and separate into three major portions, all reddish brown. The first nuclear test ever to use a plastic bonded explosive (PBX) for the implosion system.

Flathead was the first shot in Redwing detonated on a twenty-ton telemetering barge, and the blast left enormous cavities in the ocean floor. A swimming float, anchored in the lagoon with huge concrete blocks, was found floating at sea, and two of the blocks ended up in the middle of the island. Nothing remained of the boat itself—the steel didn't just melt, it burned into ash.

I was wrong when I assumed ahead of time that no matter which way we faced, one of the blasts would be in front of us. That didn't happen. But, with thirty-two aircraft participating, the Flathead cloud rose to a height of 60,000 feet and heavily contaminated the northern islands of Bikini. Not to mention that other atoll.

Welcome to Fallout Number Three.

LITOBORA

―――――⚛―――――

DURING THE BLACKHEAD FALLOUT, I MANAGED (AT FIRST) NOT TO CONCENTRATE on what was going on around me. And inside me. Instead I focused on Major Maxwell's latest grim joke. After fallout number two, he instructed everyone to stay out of the rain (despite his insistence that there were no fallouts). His order, of course, was impossible to follow since it rained all the time on The Rock.

And what about the movies? Did they stop the film at the start of the nightly downpour and tell everyone to get inside? What do you think! And did the men rush off their wooden benches and head for cover? Right again! Not even radiation and the fear of permanent genetic damage could keep the crowds away. The boredom of the present, I suppose, was worse than the cancers of the future.

I sat in the depot office and listened to the clicking and thought about the people who had inhabited the island before me. The Spanish who discovered the Marshalls in the 1600s. The Germans who established a protectorate in 1886. The Japanese, a World War I ally of ours, who took over in 1914—their authority made "official" later in the Treaty of Versailles.

The World War II battle for Eniwetok took place in February 1944, and Gen. Yoshima Nishida ordered his troops to fight to the death. 2,677 Japanese soldiers obliged, and they were buried under what was now the airport runway, close to the depot office, graves beneath the wheels of our bombers. Their spirits surrounded me every day, and I wondered if they were laughing too at Major Maxwell's grim joke. Or laughing at us. Taking revenge with their ghostly grins. Knowing we were the men in danger now while they were safe, immune to the poisons we had brought to their resting place, which was not so restful after all.

I thought about the burial ground of the Eniwetok natives at the southern end of the island, not too far from the depot, not too near the Japanese. These men and women believed the souls of the dead were released from the earth when fresh white coral was placed next to their graves. But the coral there was no longer fresh and *their* troubled spirits confronted me too, more vapor swirling around me in a concrete wasteland, more threats in the shape of a cloud.

I thought about the natives who used to live on our island (*our* island?) before their relocation to Ujelang Atoll in December 1947. Just in time to celebrate Christmas (and the Marshallese holiday *Kurijmoj*). Just in time to celebrate Operation Sandstone.

Before the move, Eniwetok was a matriarchy, with property handed down from generation to generation through the mothers. These were people who valued trees, considered them sacred. Unlike the Japanese, who cut down many of them in 1944 and aimed the trimmed trunks at the sky—in the hope the attacking Americans in their ships and planes would mistake them for artillery. Other trees burned to the ground during the battle. The rest were destroyed to make way for a test site.

Women and trees. Once important, but they didn't exist here anymore.

The Bikini natives, evacuated before the families of Eniwetok (before Operation Crossroads), were less fortunate. They were exiled to Rongerik to prevent their exposure to radiation, but there they found what they were trying to escape. Their new home was ruled by Lito-bora, the Demon of Poison.

Marshallese legends are filled with Demons who were kept at bay for generations by natives burning bright fires at night. But after we invaded their early morning darkness with a fire brighter than the sun, their magic lost its power. The former residents of Bikini became gravely ill from the fish they caught and the food they grew on Ron-gerik. Many of them died—because of Litobora.

On this day I have my own demons. I think about the colors in the fireballs and the mushroom clouds: yellow and pink and red and or-ange and blue and purple. Radioactive particles out there with my name written all over them, headed straight for me and ready to pen-etrate my bloodstream, ready to alter my life forever.

I face the specter of an assaulting spectrum. A nuclear rainbow attempting to destroy me. My enemy: Litobora.

Can I survive?

ANIMALS ON THE PATIO

I RETURNED TO MY OLD ALMA MATER, THE SNAKEPIT, FOR ONLY THE SECOND TIME since graduation. On this evening, I intended to get totally, completely and absolutely annihilated.

One step through the door and I was reminded once again there was more noise and frenzy here than anywhere else on The Rock. I made my way to the stand-up bar, where men bought beer and hard liquor. I got in line and after a while the guy behind me elbowed me in the ribs. Letting me know it was my turn to order.

"A martini," I said, putting my money on the bar.

"Asshole!" the bartender yelled at me.

I corrected myself. "Gin on the rocks."

"Gin and ice," he snarled and handed me my drink in an Eniwetok cocktail glass—a paper cup. (The beer drinkers didn't get glasses *or* cups, only beer cans.)

I was about to sit when I noticed the chair had a coating of dried vomit. The cleaning standards had gone down! I chose one that was cleaner (if not clean). Somebody else took my rejected chair, then sang along with the hillbilly tune playing on the jukebox, the eardrum-shattering volume of which was permanently cranked up to the highest level.

I looked around me. Two men (at different tables) were crying, although no one but me seemed to notice. At least half a dozen others were silent and booze-dazed and staring off into space. Two guys were arguing (loudly) over who was going to put the next coin in the jukebox, but their dispute ended abruptly when one of them collapsed on the filthy floor and passed out. Elsewhere men fought (with fists) over who was next in the bar line, and three men chased a fourth around the room and goosed him, the only exception to the no-touching taboo and the only place on The Rock where it occurred.

At the table next to me, someone was mumbling: "I want a piece of ass. I want to get laid. I hate it here. I want to get out of this place. Whoever I am, please help me."

Snakepit, ye olde atomic pub, you were the drinking place of the twentieth century.

I went to the outside patio, where it was quieter. Without walls to contain and amplify the noise, the sound dissolved and evaporated into the evening sky, sliding away softly, lost across the Pacific. This was the highest spot on the island, a few feet above sea level and surrounded by a railing. Just beyond, rocks descended gradually to the lagoon below. Dazzling sunsets filled the sky, and after dark the lights from the club reflected on the calm surface with a peaceful glow.

The men on the patio were easier to ignore. Mostly they were cardplayers who didn't say much, and when they did, their volume was not turned up as loud as it would go, like the jukebox and the men inside. I looked at the water and studied the patterns of the lights close to shore. Then I looked off into the distance where the Pacific was black. Like me.

I sat down and cased the joint. And I saw Carl Duncan. Who didn't drink. Until Penny met someone new. He was drinking now, and we were going to be an odd pair of drinking buddies. The blind drunk leading the blind drunk.

I watched Carl gulp his beverage and place the empty cup on the small round table in front of him alongside four other cups. Then he carefully fit them inside each other, admired his creation for a moment and pounded them with his fist until they were flat and broken. Crushed, the way he himself looked.

I was about to go back inside for a second Eniwetok Martini when Carl stopped me. Not that he had even seen me yet. Not that he would have recognized me in his current condition even if his face had been pointed in my direction.

Carl stopped me with his blank stare and the wooden way he moved. I watched him lean over and pet Hula with an odd, jerky motion and then feed her a piece of cheese. Buddy and Gizmo trotted over and Carl offered them cheese too, but they rejected the offering— preoccupied at the moment with their noses at Hula's tail. Carl gave the second piece to Hula, who rewarded him by licking his hand. Carl picked her up, put her in his lap and tickled her stomach. Buddy and Gizmo wandered off.

Carl stretched out his legs and slouched in his seat and, in his new position, forced Hula to the ground. He lowered his hand and stroked her absently, first her head, then her body. He gave her more cheese, and she thanked him by putting a paw on his leg. Just then Buddy bounded over to Hula again.

I had a feeling something terrible was going to happen. And I am not someone who has premonitions.

This vague sense of impending disaster was triggered by the memory of Frenchy, who looked like Hula. I watched Carl and Hula and thought about the afternoon I was fifteen years old, the last day I saw our terrier. More images from the past that I wanted to keep buried. I squinted my eyes hard, trying to drive them away.

And then I looked at Carl again. Transfixed, as I watched him stare at the dogs, who nipped at each other playfully. And I saw him pound the paper cups once more with his fist.

At this moment, Buddy and Gizmo sniffed Hula again, and Carl rose from his chair abruptly and stumbled, barely able to keep his balance. He raised his arms and muttered: "Those dogs! They've got it made!"

He bent down, heavy with the weight of alcohol and unhappiness, and wrapped his hands gently around Hula. He picked her up and cradled her in his arms. He was crying and his tears dripped down onto the dog's mangy coat. Hula sniffed Carl's chest and then stretched up and licked his face, and Carl patted her head again.

Carl stood up straight now and, holding Hula in his arms, stumbled/lurched over to the railing, looked out into the lagoon, and yelled: "They've got it made! Those dogs have got it made!"

His voice was loud enough to make the drinkers and cardplayers stop and look over.

"What the fuck is that asshole doing!" a short, fat man shouted out. A young, round-faced, curly-haired drinker asked no one in particular: "Why doesn't somebody stop him?"

I was frozen as I watched Carl, and I remembered Frenchy wandering around the apartment that last afternoon. During those months, the nurse tried to keep Fraulein sedated whenever she was not actually getting shock treatments, but on that particular day Fraulein was awake and she recognized me. She cried and told me how unhappy she was without me. She told me Frenchy was her only friend in the world.

I saw Carl lift Hula above his head. He reached over the railing and hurled her as high and as far as he could. Hula yelped in shock and traveled a few feet up and a few yards out and sailed through the air with legs twisted in every direction. A grotesque grace. Head strangely slanted. Open jaw biting the wind.

And I remembered Fraulein telling me that afternoon that she wanted to strangle me for leaving her. And when the nurse left the room, Fraulein took Frenchy in her arms and probably petted her and let the dog lick her face. And then she put her hands around Frenchy's neck and tightened her fingers.

I watched Hula miss the rocks below and land in the water. Frantic paws and furious paddling in the cold nighttime lagoon. Swimming and struggling hard to reach shore and keep from going under. Frightened and shivering. I wondered if Hula was going to make it.

And I thought about the afternoon Fraulein strangled our dog-child until she was dead. I was home but I didn't find out what happened to Frenchy until long after that day. Nobody wanted to upset me, I was told later. All I knew then was that Frenchy was not there anymore.

Soon it would be Fraulein's turn. Within the hour, an ambulance came to our building and the medics took Fraulein to a mental hospital. I watched her being carried out of the apartment on a stretcher. (Did anyone think *that* wouldn't upset me?)

Another monumental hole in my life and a caustic mixture of sadness and relief. And why in the world was I only thinking of *me*?

After that day, I was never to see Fraulein again.

I watched Hula struggle to get to land, and finally she made it. She crawled onto the rocks down below and shook off the water.

Carl watched too and emitted a laugh: primitive, deranged, out of control. He bent over and yanked Buddy from the ground. Buddy barked and tried to get away but Carl held on to him.

"They've got it made!" he shouted one more time. His yell was followed by a dark, half-strangled sound coming from deep in his chest. A sort of low moan. Men on Eniwetok were always making strange guttural noises, frequently followed by unintelligible syllables.

Carl's eyes were haunted and intense, and he was holding Buddy over his head the way he had held Hula. I ran toward them.

"Put Buddy down!" I shouted. Carl didn't react. I yelled again and raced to get to him in time to pull the dog from his hands. But I didn't have to. This time he heard me and he did put down the dog. He dropped Buddy hard. With a thud. Then he cackled shrilly at some private joke and dropped himself to the ground. With a thud.

"Get up!" I ordered. "We're getting out of here!"

I didn't know if he'd be able to, but he did what I said and my own loud voice seemed to sober him a little.

We stood outside the Snakepit and he apologized. "For everything," he said. I was surprised he wasn't slurring his words. Once I realized he would actually be able to understand what I was saying, I told him I had just gotten my own Dear John letter so now I knew exactly how he felt. And it wasn't pleasant.

"As a matter of fact, you don't know how I feel," he said lucidly. And he was not being argumentative. "I didn't level with you. I didn't tell you the worst part."

And I thought: What could possibly be worse than losing the only woman you've ever loved?

"I told you that Penny met someone new," he said.

"And that isn't true?"

"It's true all right, but it's not what's really bothering me now."

His face was scarred by conflict and anguish. I waited for him to say more, to explain, but he was silent. He told me he wasn't ready to talk about it yet. Maybe he'd never be ready. But if and when he was, he'd let me know.

All he would say about himself at that moment was fourteen words: "The real problem is that I'VE met someone new. Right here. On The Rock."

THE MORNING BREAK

BILLY BYRNE WAS EATING A DOUGHNUT IN A SHED NEXT TO THE SUPPLY DEPOT, where an urn of coffee and doughnuts were brought from the mess hall every morning at 9:30. He was holding the first of three that he consumed each day during the half-hour coffee break, and he would have eaten more if the men didn't stop him. If he had been allowed to satisfy his appetites, there wouldn't have been enough to go around for everyone else.

Billy Byrne was in the middle of doughnut number one when Hawkins decided to satisfy his own appetites—and there was more than enough of Billy Byrne to go round. Hawkins grabbed him from behind and took him by surprise. The uneaten half of the first doughnut fell to the ground.

Two and a half to go but not today, Billy Byrne. I'm putting you to better use.

Billy Byrne fought back. He tried to land blows with his fist and open hands. He aimed at every part of Hawkins within reach, but all he did was toss his arms around wildly. He wasn't quick enough or strong enough to defend himself. And he had to watch out for the razor blade.

On this fucking island, you gotta take what you want. And if you don't know how to do that, you're nowhere.

Billy Byrne never stopped struggling. Once he broke away, but Hawkins caught him and "taught him a lesson" by punching him hard in the stomach. Where most of him was. Not in the chest because Hawkins wasn't going to damage the merchandise.

You gotta make your own fun out here. Nobody's going to do it for you. All you're going to get from anyone else is radiation and fallout.

Before the coffee break was over, Hawkins the outlaw got what he wanted.

Billy Byrne couldn't imagine the same demands would be made of him on the following morning. And on mornings after that.

For men on The Rock, the long long year was filled with hopeless moments. For Billy Byrne, one of those hopeless moments came at the end of that week, at the beginning of the morning break when Hawkins reached for him again. Billy Byrne reached the breaking point. And went beyond.

He cried. His entire body shook and trembled. He looked like a man having convulsions, and his sobs sounded like screams.

Hawkins went ahead anyway, but Billy Byrne's shaking and crying ruined his pleasure. And then there was Captain Weiss and Major Vanish, who always remained in the depot during coffee break. Billy Byrne was making so much noise they might wonder if somebody was being tortured. And if they came outside and saw what was going on, they might not like it.

So Hawkins let Billy Byrne go.

Billy Byrne went back inside the depot after coffee break. Still crying and shaking. Captain Weiss was not there, and that meant this was one of those rare occasions when Major Vanish had to handle a situation on his own.

"Are you feeling okay?" he asked Billy Byrne. Although it was obvious he wasn't.

Billy Byrne (still shaking) shrugged.

"Maybe you're catching a cold," Major Vanish said. "Why don't you go back to the barracks? There's nothing so important here today that we can't do without you for a few hours."

So Major Vanish did what Hawkins had done earlier. He let Billy Byrne go. Still weeping and trembling as he left the depot and made his way back to the barracks.

Where Tony found him later that morning.

Headquarters Company, where Tony did his typing, was located inside one of a semicircular cluster of buildings that faced the ocean. These structures—square, rectangular and L-shaped—had their entrances on the ocean side. In front was a path and next to it, a concrete "park" with nothing in it, and the two were separated by a row of stones painted white. By unspoken agreement, soldiers followed their own strange self-imposed rule and walked only on the path—to avoid trampling the imaginary grass.

The rear of these buildings faced the main drag of the island, its Broadway. This was "downtown Eniwetok," the center of local activity, and from there it was a five-minute walk to the PX, the mess hall, the I&E office—and to the barracks, where Tony went late that morning to change his bandages.

He walked with a limp, a temporary souvenir of the bullet wound, and he moved carefully as he made his way down the long quiet corridor, his eyes searching the cement floor for anything that could trip him. The barracks were always empty at this hour, when everyone was at work, but as Tony approached our room, he sensed he was not alone. And then he looked up. He saw a pair of shoes dangling in midair. Feet suspended in space, defying gravity.

He rushed forward. An aloha shirt hanging from a ceiling beam. A head hanging from the aloha shirt. A torso swinging. And noises coming from a throat: gurgling sounds.

Billy Byrne waiting for death. Waiting for the weight of his body to kill him.

Tony grabbed the chair Billy Byrne had used earlier when he placed the aloha noose around his neck and now, dragging a gimpy leg, stood on it himself. Tony lifted the heavy body with one arm, loosened the shirt from around the neck with his free hand, stepped down and, sweating, lugged a limp Billy Byrne across the room.

"Are you crazy!" Tony said, dumping him on his bed.

The response was more choking sounds, followed by sputtering, followed by silence. And finally Billy Byrne's words: "What did you do that for? I would have been better off."

"Like hell you would."

More silence from Billy Byrne.

Tony: "Did you ever stop and think how much your mother would miss you?"

Billy Byrne shook his head. "No."

"Then start thinking about it now."

Without a phone or an intercom, the only way to get assistance was to go to the hospital, as Duncan found out after Wilson pulled the trigger. Billy Byrne seemed out of danger now—except by his own hands—but that was reason enough not to leave him alone. Tony yelled for help, hoping somebody would hear, but the only response was an echo.

"Take it easy," Tony said, aware the lunchtime mob would descend in a little while. "The medics will check you out soon."

Tony waited, keeping an eye on Billy Byrne as he looked around the room. He noticed scraps of paper on the floor held together with Scotch tape and he recognized the lined yellow tablet sheets and the penciled words, all in capitals. Letters from Billy Byrne's mother that Eder had ripped up months before—now a giant reconstructed jigsaw puzzle.

Tony read a few words silently: "I know it's hard for you in the army but try and be strong and try not to cry. Take my word, one of these days the boys in your barracks will understand you are speshal [*sic*], just the way I do."

"You put the pages back together," Tony said, looking up at Billy Byrne.

"Yeah."

"Those letters must mean a lot to you."

"Yeah," said Billy Byrne. Then he burst into sobs. "They're from my Mommadee."

. . .

At lunch hour, several men escorted Billy Byrne to the hospital, and that afternoon Tony learned for the first time what had been going on. Craig described The Big Feel that Hawkins had organized in the barracks and Straletti told him what happened at the depot.

"Hawkins wouldn't leave him alone," Straletti said.

"Billy Byrne didn't fight back?"

"He tried to, but you know Billy Byrne. He's not good at it. He made an effort and just gave up."

"And that went on every day?" Tony asked.

Straletti nodded. "During coffee break. Today was the worst. Billy Byrne just shook and cried. The major sent him back to the barracks."

"And Hawkins was the only one?"

Craig nodded. "Nobody else would have anything to do with it. We were all kind of disgusted."

Tony said nothing. Showed no reaction. His first comment came when Hawkins returned to the barracks after work. Tony spoke to him with a silent fist in the gut.

Hawkins backed away. Raised his arms and turned them into a white flag. Terror invaded his face—only Tony did that to him. Hawkins said nothing but his eyes wanted to know: What was that all about?

Tony answered in the other language. "You don't understand? You've got ten seconds to figure it out. And if you have any trouble, ask Billy Byrne."

Hawkins made a dash for the door. But Tony grabbed him by the shoulder, spun him around with his left hand, and landed a right fist hard to the jaw. Blood trickled from Hawkins's mouth and he staggered, doubled over in pain.

Tony raised his fist again, about to strike another time. Hawkins tried to lift his arms and protect himself. He was dazed and barely able to. Tony's knuckles landed in his right eye. Twice.

Men from other rooms heard the groans and the sounds of flesh pounding flesh, and they gathered at the door, watched, said nothing. Billy Byrne, back from the hospital, was there too and silent, but his mouth was turned up in a faint smile.

Tony continued. Eyes, cheeks, mouth—all bloody. Hawkins stood with his arms at his sides. Perhaps afraid that fighting back would only make it worse. Perhaps unable to fight anymore.

Tony worked his way down—chest, stomach, ribs. Hawkins blinked and stumbled and his hands reached out, as if he were grabbing on to air to hold himself up.

And then Tony stopped and went back to words again. "What are you going to do to Billy Byrne in the future?"

"Nothing." Almost inaudible.

"I can't hear you. Speak up."

"Nothing."

"You're going to leave him alone," Tony said. "Right?"

Hawkins, barely able to nod and speak, did both: "I'm going to leave him alone."

Tony connected with one last blow to the gut, more powerful than the others. A final punctuation mark that sent Hawkins to the floor.

Billy Byrne chuckled. Tony turned around and glared at him: "What do *you* find so funny?"

"Nothing," Billy Byrne mumbled.

"I'm warning you," Tony said. "Don't ever *think* about repeating this morning's performance."

"I won't. I promise." He looked and sounded truly regretful.

And then Billy Byrne turned away. Tony couldn't see that the faint smile on his face was back again. This time more pronounced.

A look of victory, I thought.

PART SIX

Surviving

FAREWELL PRESENT

THE THREE HORSEMEN WERE THROWN FROM THEIR HORSES.

Hawkins metamorphosed once again after his encounter with Tony. He stopped carrying a razor blade and found yet another way to pass the time and fight off the boredom. He sketched. Drawings of dead men hanging from ropes. Blind men with empty holes where their eyes used to be. Then he came across photographs of Japanese damaged by the bombs at Hiroshima and Nagasaki and found the theme he had been searching for. He made pictures of children covered with skin lesions. Adults with faces and bodies ravaged by scarred flesh and pain.

Noonen was now a follower without a leader, and he found a way to fill the gap. He discovered religion. Noonen, the follower, followed God. Went to church every Sunday and talked about God's vengeance every day. And volunteered to work as a chaplain's helper in his free time.

Noonen had said on the morning before the first explosion: "Maybe we won't live through the test. Maybe this will be our last day." Now he crossed himself when he read articles about the H-bomb. Closed his eyes when other men voiced their fears. Said "Amen" anytime someone was the least bit hopeful.

Eder had also played Follow the Leader, but *his* change occurred when his Magic Number hit fourteen and he got "shook," a condition that afflicted almost all the men in the weeks before they left The Rock. They were not excited or agitated as the word might imply but lost in a private world, not talking, not responding to men who talked to *them.*

A silent Eder stayed on his bed frozen in one position. And he never exercised. I told him to do sit-ups again or his muscles would turn to flab and no broad in the States would look at him. I'm sure he never heard me or anyone else he was sharing the planet with. He looked off into space with blank eyes. The Kilmer Look, Eniwetok's good old Staring Disease, but this time the familiar virus had a different cause.

Tony was leaving the island on the same day as Eder, but he was one of the few people I knew on The Rock who didn't get "shook." I assumed Irene's uncertain condition (there were frequent bulletins) provided the antidote to the usual departure symptom. I knew he was thinking about her and writing to her daily.

But at least the heart palpitations and shortness of breath were gone. I had recently remembered that a college classmate of mine had the same symptoms. The diagnosis was panic attacks, and I was willing to bet that was Tony's problem too. Former problem. Not that he had any less to panic about now.

Several days before Tony and Eder were scheduled to leave, the army gave them a going-away present.

As usual, we got up before dawn. On other mornings, men bitched about not getting enough sleep. Not today—everyone was relaxed. No postponements to push nerves to the limit. No monster bomb (or even one close in size), so no worries about being vaporized. The weather appeared ideal (not that any of us had a direct pipeline to the Greatest Weather-Forecasting System in History). And there was not going to be an air drop—no pilot and flight crew to mistake an observation facility on the wrong island for the targeting beacon.

Test Number Nine, code name Kickapoo, was going to be a plain, simple, uncomplicated, ordinary burst. The device, known as Swallow, was a UCRL linear implosion design intended for air defense warheads and was placed on a stationary three-hundred-foot-tall tower on Aomon (Sally) Island, Eniwetok Atoll. No moving parts to malfunction. No question about the location of the blast. No possibility anything could go wrong.

We marched to the lagoon and stood at attention, our backs to the explosion, our faces naked as always. It was still before sunrise, and the sky was black. We listened to the Disembodied Voice broadcast the countdown.

Four.

Three.

Two.

One.

Zero.

Explosion.

And even though my eyes were closed and my arm was shielding my face, a brilliant light penetrated my eyelids. The world was brighter now than it had ever been, brighter than it was during Cherokee, the monster bomb.

I felt knives behind my eyes and they gouged the inside of my head. Sharp thin pieces of steel twisted around and invaded nerves and tissues in the middle of my skull. I had never felt pain so excruciating, and I was amazed I was not screaming. Or was I?

Estabrook was standing to my right and I heard a deep, low-pitched sound of agony come from his gut. I knew then I was not the only one. Estabrook felt the knives too.

I heard a voice I did not recognize: "Oh, no!"

I heard: "Shit!" (sounded like Carl Duncan).

I heard a groan: "Ohhhhh." Hawkins.

I heard praying and cursing and screaming.

I didn't understand what was happening. What had gone wrong today?

And then (like the pain) the answer hit me behind the eyes. For the second time, the D.V. was not going to tell us to turn around. No need. I had just figured out that ground zero was right there in front of us. Again. This time there was no pilot to blame, so who screwed up? Who had us facing the wrong direction? Who put us face to face with another hydrogen bomb? I didn't know. Yet. But I was able to make a pretty shrewd guess.

Minutes passed and the D.V. said we could open up our eyes. If you believed in prayer, you prayed then that when you did, you would be able to see out of them. I did not believe in prayer, but I prayed anyway. My silent plea took a few seconds, and I opened my eyes. I could see. I looked around and saw men on their knees pounding the ground with their fists. I saw men lying flat on their backs with their mouths open in silent screams. I saw men with their palms over their eyes and their screams were not silent. I saw men doubled over. I saw men holding their heads, their hands shielding their eyes. I saw men on the ground curled in the fetal position, begging for the pain to stop.

I saw a battlefield, and we were on the losing side.

The officers were not screaming or crying or moaning or pounding the ground with their fists. They were removing their goggles.

The rest of us wondered: Was Redwing removing our sight?

We thought about the future. Would our tears pour out of glass eyes one day?

The D.V. told us we could talk again. The same words the MP corporal had used before we left the briefing room on the afternoon we arrived. Again, nobody did.

Why these symptoms today and not during Cherokee? Something about the angle of the fireball, according to the scientists. And ground zero being so much closer to Eniwetok Island. That meant the potential damage was more severe. If men without goggles were facing the blast.

Why *was* ground zero in front of us? Major Maxwell gathered us together to explain:

"You win a few and you lose a few and sometimes things don't turn out the way you want. When that happens, you take it on the chin like a man and start all over again."

His uniform, always pressed and spotless, was rumpled today, and there was a dark stain on his shorts. His socks were not rolled. In fact, he was not even wearing socks.

"Things happen in this world and you can't let them get to you. The secret is to look at the positive side."

His rodent-colored hair, on other days short and carefully trimmed, was long. Unruly tufts protruded in every direction.

"Be vigilant or be dead! *I* know that and the *army* knows that and *you* know that. We're not going to let them throw us a curve."

His eyes weren't quite focused. And he stuttered—I had never heard him do that before.

"Furthermore, Rujoru and Yurochi. And more important, Aomon is Sally and not Ruby. Not as easy as you think. And that's the way things are."

I put to use one of my Rock-acquired skills: an ability to translate Maxwellese into ordinary English. MM was saying the explosion was in front of us because he had gotten confused about the location of ground zero. He knew Rujoru was Pearl and Yurochi was Dog. But he thought Aomon Island was Ruby when it was really Sally. He was telling us it was much more difficult than we might imagine to keep every name straight when each island had two.

Why two? "To prevent confusion," according to the army, but now I knew the real reason. So the major could make sure that all of us faced the fireball.

WHITE CHRISTMAS

I WAS TWENTY-THREE BUT I FELT MYSELF GETTING OLD. MY NIGHTMARES STARTED after this test, Number Nine.

In one, a classic chase scene, I was running and my pursuer was getting closer and closer. Catching up to me. I knew I could not survive unless I forced more speed from my legs. And then, just as the hunter reached forward to grab me, I was able to sprint. I put distance between me and this strange shadow of mine. Only then did I turn around to find out who was after me. And I saw I was being chased by a mushroom cloud—yellow and pink and red and orange and blue and purple. I screamed. And when I woke up, I was still running and screaming.

In another dream, I had X-ray eyes. I stared at my hands and saw bones. I examined my legs: more bones. I was a walking skeleton. I looked hollow and I felt hollow but I inspected myself in a mirror and I found out I was not as empty as I imagined. I observed my lungs and kidneys and liver and heart. And next to them, tiny mysterious specks (not part of me) glowed in the dark. I watched them attack my body and saw the contents of my skin shrivel up, become dry and lifeless, grapes turning into raisins. And I knew then what the specks were: organ grinders.

In one more dream, a hand was about to touchpresspush a large crimson button, the color of my own blood. And if I could not stop that from happening, the planet was going to shatter into countless small fragments. But I was unable to move. My hand was paralyzed and so was the rest of me. No part of my body could move except for my eyes. And slowly they closed.

In the worst nightmare, we were lined up in formation. After "zero," there was the bright blinding light and the sound and the shock wave—wild winds pushing back the skin on my face, blowing off the hat I was not wearing, knocking me to the ground. I waited for more to happen, and I knew what was coming next. I was going to be refreshed by small gritty hail-like particles that would fall on top of me. The same inch-thick "snow" the Marshallese children had played in during Castle Bravo. Before they had to have their thyroid nodules surgically removed. Before they "rapidly recovered."

That was the White Christmas I was dreaming of.

"ANYTHING BUT
BROKEN HEARTS"

CARL DUNCAN TOLD ME HE HAD NEVER BEEN EXCITED BY A MAN'S BODY BEFORE
Operation Redwing—another way of saying the H-Bomb made him
gay (although we used the word "homosexual" in those days). To me,
that was an incredible statement. I didn't believe it, though I had no
trouble believing he was upset.

"You'll feel better if you talk about it," I told him. A cliché of the
time and a cornerstone of Richter's view of the cosmos. And also
something I believed myself back then.

Carl wasn't interested. "You wouldn't understand. It's hard for
me to understand, so how can I expect *you* will?"

"Take a chance. Try me. What have you got to lose?"

He said he would think about it, and several days later he decided
to try me. We walked to the lagoon (where he used to read his letters
from Penny), and there I discovered, to my surprise, that the H-bomb
did make him gay.

. . .

Carl said that when the tests started, he was anxious all the time, "I don't know what bothered me more, the bomb or the men who were afraid of the bomb. They both got to me, and I had trouble sleeping at night."

As the tests continued, his fears seemed justified. The pilot missed his target. A "device" exploded in front of us. Fallouts and Geiger counters became routine. Although he didn't talk about it much, he reached a point where he didn't think about anything except the H-bomb and the damage it might be causing. To him and to Penny and to their future life. That was when he started taking long walks to calm himself.

Instead of wandering through the woods the way he did in Wisconsin, he wandered along the concrete and headed toward the fat part of Eniwetok. Carl worked at Headquarters Company (in the same bull pen of typists as Tony) and he had not been down to the far end of The Rock since the day he arrived. A tiny island with not much to see, but, like most of the men stationed there, he never bothered to explore what little there was.

Carl walked down Lagoon Road past the Snakepit and came to the repair shop, one of The Rock's largest buildings, an enormous aluminum enclosure that looked like an airplane hangar and was located, appropriately, close to the airport. A sign in front said: WE FIX ANYTHING BUT BROKEN HEARTS.

He went inside and he was overpowered by the smell of sawdust and metal shavings. "I felt at home right away," he told me. "The place reminded me of my grandfathers' carpentry shed, only much much larger."

Workers with electric tools were using skills they could have been using at home, and their expressions were intense but peaceful. He had seen the same look on the faces of Uncle Lester and Uncle Carl but never on Eniwetok. The men at the repair shop seemed lost in the sheer physical pleasure of what they were doing.

He returned a few days later and realized it was the noise that helped them bury themselves inside a private world of work. The sound of the machinery was so loud that talking was impossible, and they seemed unaware of each other. They were absorbed and contented as they concentrated on what they were doing—until a moment came when Carl could see their memories intrude. He told me that all of a sudden they seemed conscious again of where they were and where they weren't.

The present (or the past) burst through and they stopped, frozen in the same position they were in when the thought first caught them. They stayed that way, rigid and immobile, and stared off into the distance, focusing on nothing in particular. Or maybe on their off-island lives. Or their island lives. After a short while, they returned to work.

"In those few minutes," he told me, "I could see clearly what the island does to the men who live here."

The repair shop was a distraction for him, and he returned whenever he could. "I was able to relax there. I knew it was an unusual way to pass the time but not as strange as what some of the other guys were doing."

Men worked outside too and Carl preferred it there—it was quieter. Without the sound of machinery echoing against aluminum walls, the hums and the whistles were lower and less shrill. The repair shop's version of the Snakepit patio. Outside, it was harder for the men to tune out The Rock and get lost in work, but they were more responsive to the people around them. Sometimes they talked and told jokes and even laughed.

In the beginning, Carl refused to admit the real reason he was drawn to the repair shop. Most of the soldiers on The Rock wore shirts: short-sleeve khakis at work and Hawaiian aloha shirts off duty. Outside at the repair shop, everyone was shirtless. Carl went there to look at dozens of well-built men naked above the waist.

"It was easy to ignore the truth because I've never done anything like that before. Or felt anything like that before. In the shower room at high school after football and baseball practice, I was surrounded by bare-assed men, but in those days the only body that interested me was Penny's. And it was the same in the army. Until Redwing."

Eventually he had to stop kidding himself—he had an erection most of the time at the repair shop. But he was sure his new feelings were temporary and after he left the island (if not sooner) he would turn back into the old, familiar Carl Duncan. For the time being, he might as well get a few harmless kicks—there were not many ways to do that on The Rock.

And so he continued walking through sawdust. Every day he stared at chests and arms and biceps and triceps and abs and thighs.

But the daily visits affected him in ways he didn't expect. The repair shop took his mind off the tests, but bare-chested men took over his mind. In the barracks, the bomb was replacing women as the main topic of conversation, but just when other men stopped thinking about sex all the time, Carl started.

He loved watching men lift and stretch and carry and bend, and he was mesmerized by the sweaty torsos glistening in the sun. Dazzled by shining bodies performing just for him under their own yellow spotlight.

In time, he began to understand his new obsession, and he wanted me to understand too.

"The bomb made me feel small. And each time a test went wrong, I felt smaller and more helpless and more afraid."

The repair shop was his antidote. He said the soldiers there were rugged and large, and looking at them made *him* feel as strong as *they* looked. His emptiness disappeared—as if he had absorbed their strength.

Comparing *his* inner feelings (powerless) with *their* outer bodies (powerful) made no sense to me. Besides, I was sure the workers at the repair shop were just as frightened of the bomb as he was, and Carl, at five-ten and 160 pounds, was no midget but a nicely built man. Although I had never seen the guys he was watching, I was willing to bet that many of them were smaller and less muscular than he was. But that was not how he perceived himself or these men.

Still, I couldn't argue with the facts. Carl stopped feeling powerless when he went to the repair shop and looked at men he thought were powerful. And somewhere along the way, that translated into physical desire.

When his fears escalated, so did his sex drive. That was how he and his body reacted to the H-bomb threat. I didn't know of anyone else who responded that way, but other soldiers had other bizarre defenses.

If Carl had been on an island with women as well as men, maybe he would have spent his time thinking about nurses and WACs. But he was on The Rock, and it was male bodies that helped keep his terrors at bay.

Back home, Carl had never heard of a man who was excited by men. And, to my surprise, not in the army either.

"It was scary believing I was the only one, and I didn't want anybody to find out."

He made sure the workers at the repair shop didn't know he was staring. He kept his right hand above his eyes as if he were shielding them from the sun, so nobody could see where they were focused. And he made himself look official by walking stiffly and briskly, head forward. He told me the men were occupied with their own chores and assumed (if they thought about it at all) that a trespasser must have a good reason for being on the premises.

One man at the repair shop intrigued Carl more than any other. He worked outside, had black black hair, a dark tan (of course) and was very large, six-three with broad shoulders. To Carl, he seemed seven feet tall.

He liked the way this man stood and walked and smiled. Carl never spoke to him but thought about him every waking moment. He turned into an addict, and each day the craving grew stronger. Soon, looking was not enough. He wanted to touch too. And the intensity of those feelings frightened him.

And yet (in a way) it was comforting and reassuring to know that his fantasies could never turn into reality. Since no one knew how he felt. And no one else felt the same way. And if somebody somewhere did, it could never be Ken Bishop, the man with the black black hair. Who was strong and powerful and very masculine.

Ken was the last man in the world who would respond. Carl had no doubt about that.

But he was wrong.

One afternoon Ken realized Carl was looking at him. And looked back. And smiled.

Carl wanted to say something but the words wouldn't come. He smiled himself and then ended the awkwardness by holding up his hand as a sort of good-bye wave. Ken nodded and Carl left.

He spent the evening trying to figure out what to say to Ken the next day. Ask him about his work? Where he was from? How long he'd been on The Rock?

But when Carl returned, he didn't have to say anything. Ken handed him a note: Meet you tonight at ten at Oceanview National Park.

Carl nodded. Ken smiled and nodded too and then turned around and went back to work.

Carl watched him and wondered how many years there were between then and ten o'clock that night.

They did meet. And not just once. I had imagined from Carl's tears and drunkenness at the Snakepit that he was consumed with guilt, but no, he was happy and comfortable with Ken. Any guilt he felt was focused only on his friend Hula.

The letter from Penny had made him fall apart because he was angry at her (not to mention his "best friend," Keith). He felt betrayed but he also felt he had betrayed *her* and didn't deserve her anymore.

After we talked he *did* feel better, and I was almost sorry about that. If he were upset, he might have been cautious. The Rock was a dangerous place for the two of them and they were juggling flames, but Carl had no intention of ending his new friendship. Ken was his novocaine. And more.

"Be careful," I told him.

"You don't have to worry about us," he said. "We *are* careful. We know what we're doing."

But so did Sam and Arthur.

FAREWELL PARTY

FOUR DAYS TO GO FOR TONY, AND HE TOLD ME AFTER MAIL CALL THAT IRENE HAD just written that her cancer was now in remission. His face exploded with a happiness and relief I had never seen before. He was barely able to talk.

She was healthy again, she said, and the doctors told her she was going to make it—no question. But she realized she had to be practical and plan for the future, so she wrote a new will and made Tony the executor and Patty's guardian. Just in case.

I told him that even if Irene lived into old age, I could still see him as a wonderful father to Patty. There was a gentleness in his voice as he spoke to me now, and I suspected children brought that out in him.

"I hope you're right," he said. "Now all I have to do is find a girl-friend!"

I didn't point out that for Moviestar it was not going to be difficult.

Then his face changed and he looked reflective, almost sad. "I've been thinking a lot about cruelty and suffering lately. Ever since Irene got sick but before then too. You asked me why I lunged at Wilson and broke my rule about getting involved, and I wasn't completely honest with you. I said it was instinct, but it was more than that. I saw where Wilson was pointing his rifle. It was not at Billy Byrne's legs or arms or shoulders. Wilson was aiming at his heart. Whatever I thought about Billy Byrne then or now, I wasn't going to let him die."

There was nothing funny about what he said, but I smiled. "Who'd have guessed you'd end up being a hero. A double hero, since you saved his life twice."

"I had an investment to protect," Tony said.

And he smiled for what I figured was just about the fourth time since I'd known him. And it was flattering. The toughness and the hardness disappeared from his face.

Major Maxwell had said there were only two ways a man could leave The Rock—after his twelve-month tour of duty was over or in a body bag (like Geezer). So I was more than surprised when Estabrook told me that in a few days he was going back to the States for an early discharge—after three months on Eniwetok.

How come? Some very good lobbying back in Colorado. His wife had argued that it was a financial hardship not having her husband home to support the family. In those days, draftees with children had a good case. And it didn't hurt that Estabrook's congressman was a friend of his wife's parents.

Good for him. I was sure he had fought hard for this the way he did for everything else. Estabrook didn't know how to give up.

He confirmed that again on the day before his departure (he was leaving on the same plane as Tony and Eder). We planned a farewell party for the three of them that night at the Snakepit, and after work Estabrook gave me a farewell present—a tube of Naval Jelly.

"We'll go to the depot before the party," he said. "We'll put it on all the hinges, and the next time there's a fallout, you'll be able to enjoy it!"

When I recovered from the surprise, I thanked him.

At his suggestion, we started our project at the window nearest my desk. He squeezed jelly onto the aluminum hinge and pulled the window. Nothing happened.

"What is this shit?" he said. And then: "Go outside and push."

I followed his instructions, he counted to three and he pulled and I pushed at the same time.

"The fucker still won't budge," Estabrook said.

We tried a second window. No difference. Then he took a closer look at the hinges.

"The God damn fuckers are all pitted. Holes in them. This crappy aluminum is too thin and too light. Steel you could hammer, but this aluminum is a corroded piece of shit!"

We pushed and pulled other windows. We used a thicker coating of jelly. The results were always the same and sometimes worse than the same. Occasionally the jelly made the holes larger.

"They're out to screw us," Estabrook said.

And so it seemed. No matter what we did, the windows remained in place—open enough to let in every one of those radioactive particles that were out to get us.

"At least we tried," I said.

"Trying isn't good enough. I'll look around in Colorado. If I find something I think will work, I'll mail it to you."

"Let's go to the Snakepit now," I suggested. "And thank your wife for sending the Naval Jelly when you see her." I added: "In a few days." Failing to conceal the depths of my envy.

"Yes, the Snakepit. I don't know about you, but I'm going to get totally obliterated."

I didn't know about me either, but I considered that a good possibility.

I started off with Eniwetok martinis and, as far as I could tell, nobody else was drinking anything milder.

Berko with scotch (in his hand and going to his head quickly) told us that his mother had just found out he was married. She uncovered his secret when she spotted a letter from Berko to Stephanie in the lobby of their apartment building. Naturally, Mrs. Berkowitz opened it. Was she outraged that he had married a shiksa? And without telling her? Anything else would have been inconceivable to Berko. So what happened? She gave him the surprise of his life. She was *so* happy. Her daughter-in-law was a fine young woman, and she and

Berko and Berko's father (who I never knew existed until this moment) were all very lucky. He couldn't have found a nicer girl anywhere. And as long as her grandkids were brought up Jewish, there was no problem as far as *she* was concerned. ("I haven't mentioned this yet to my new daughter-in-law, but it would be very nice if she converted.")

We were all very happy for Berko (we thought), but he said his mother was still slightly irritated over the whole incident and said he deserved what she used to call a "Go to your room" when he was a child. Some sort of punishment (not as serious as a spanking) to make certain a transgression was not overlooked. She wrote him that he had done something wrong (to *her*) and even though he was an adult now, they both needed to acknowledge that. So on principle and just to make her point, she was not going to bake any cookies for him for a week.

The announcement was greeted with mock groans of disappointment. Except from Eder. Of the three departing guests of honor, he was in the worst shape by far and, if possible, more "shook" than ever. So comatose that he made Jason Underwood, also in attendance, appear vibrant by comparison. Eder now had an advanced case of the Kilmer Look. I wondered if this was the first sign that another new species was about to emerge.

The alcohol and the festivities forced an occasional sentence from Eder's mouth. He mumbled about how much he missed Wilson and pulled over an empty chair, which he told us was "Wilson's chair."

Tony said he heard Wilson had a new home and a new job. He got a medical discharge and was now a permanent resident of a VA hospital, where he was also employed as . . . Tony paused and everyone guessed correctly.

Hawkins was present but silent. He sketched mutilated men in the small notebook he kept in his back pocket (like Richter). He averted his eyes from Billy Byrne. Looked at Tony warily. Cowering—a dog fearful of another beating.

The *real* dogs present, Buddy, Hula and Gizmo, had long ago forgiven Carl and during the evening there were plenty of hugs and kisses between them. Richter announced to no one in particular that "Memories are short when you're a canine."

Carl told us a navy friend of his from the Snakepit, and the man's shipmates, had been at the Proving Ground for other tests. He said that during Operation Greenhouse, a high-ranking army officer, offended by the dozens of rusting tanks and ships surrounding Eniwetok, issued orders for all of them to be painted—a full-time job for every man on the island for a very long while. This officer was relieved of duty immediately and shipped back to the States. Presumably in the Eniwetok equivalent of a straitjacket.

Berko's comment: "Remind you of anyone we know?"

Everybody roared with laughter.

Estabrook, true to his word, did become obliterated and gave a hilarious imitation of the D.V. warning everyone to close up the sky during the fallout and not open it again until the all-clear announcement.

The evening wouldn't have been complete without one cosmic announcement from Noonen (who was mixing bourbon with beer as he browsed through his Bible).

"I'm going to get even after I leave here," Noonen said. His new feelings for God had not diminished the paranoia.

"Who with?" Berko asked.

"Who doesn't matter. I'm going on record now and telling you that someday someone is going to pay for making me hang around here watching H-bombs."

Berko: "I'm glad you're waiting until *after* you leave."

"Are you making fun of me?"

Nobody responded to the question.

By the time we closed up the Snakepit, no one was able to stand on his own. But no one had to. We headed back to the barracks together singing "Auld Lang Syne," lurching along and holding each other up.

Not unusual for drunken buddies all over the world, but something I had never witnessed before on The Rock.

OCEANVIEW NATIONAL PARK

THE BENCH FACED THE PACIFIC, AND IN FRONT OF IT A BEACH SLOPED DOWN gently to the water and leveled off. Spiny, olive green coral extended from the ocean up to the shoreline and onto the sand, covered with the shells of black snails and yellow-speckled rock lobsters.

White-tipped waves broke fiercely on the outer rim of the coral reef, and the fins of large sharks glided slowly above the foam close to land. The tides and currents were powerful, and a short way out the water was six hundred feet deep. Even the super-swimmer of the day, Johnny Weissmuller, Olympic gold medalist and star of twelve Tarzan films, could not have made it back to shore.

Next to the bench was a sign that identified this place: OCEANVIEW NATIONAL PARK.

Despite the sharks and the violent ocean, this was a peaceful spot during the day. Carl Duncan went there at night. Including the night after our conversation about Ken.

There was no moon that evening—so dark outside that when he arrived he could not see if Ken was there yet.

He called out: "Hello? Anyone here?"

Silence.

He tried again: "Hello."

Still no response.

He looked at his watch (with hands that glowed in the dark) and saw he was early. He sat down and waited.

Seconds later, he was blinded by a strong beam of light. A man in front of him shined a flashlight at his face. "What are you doing here?" a gravelly voice demanded to know.

Carl shielded his eyes from the brightness with his right arm, fireball style. "Nothing."

An angry order came back: "Just answer the question."

"Nothing. I just wanted a little peace and quiet."

The speaker turned his beam to the ground and Carl could make out a second man standing next to him. He could also see guns and billy clubs and knew for sure now what he had only guessed. MPs.

The interrogator was fat with a shaved head and spoke roughly: "Nobody sits alone in the dark in front of a fucking beach facing the ocean. You're here to meet someone."

"No, I'm not." Carl raised his voice. To warn Ken.

Fatso, laughing: "Maybe you came here to swim." His partner remained mute. "If you want to, be my guest. I'll bet you're hot as a pistol thinking about the piece of ass you were waiting for. You want to cool off, jump right in."

"I'm here alone," Carl said.

Fatso: "Only because *we* showed up. Who were you saying 'Hello' to?"

"No one." Carl was sweating and shaking. Afraid Ken would arrive at any moment. *Don't come. Please don't come.*

Fatso, getting angrier: "Do I have to ask again? Who were you talking to?"

Carl, louder: "You mean when I got here?"

"Yes. When you said hello."

Carl hunted frantically for an explanation. "I heard a lot of noise. I wondered who was out there. It turned out to be *you.*"

The silent MP, a tall thin beanpole, nodded his head, agreeing they had not been quiet enough.

That encouraged Carl to be more aggressive. "How come you were creeping around on the beach anyway?"

Fatso: "Looking for fags is our job, that's why. We're going to hang around and see what happens. Turn off our flashlights. Stop talking. Wait for your buddy to show up."

The fat man turned off his flashlight. The silent seconds passed. Carl panicked and coughed. Another warning for Ken. Then more coughing.

Fatso (trying to whisper): "Stop that!"

Carl (shouting): "I can't." He continued to cough.

Fatso: "I told you to stop."

And the fat man's fist landed in Carl's stomach. It didn't hurt but he moaned. And kept it up.

Then the beanpole spoke for the first time: "Look, Butch, we gotta get outta here pretty soon."

Butch: "You're right, Falco. We still got plenty of buildings to check out."

Butch turned on his flashlight and pointed it at Carl: "You got lucky tonight. If your buddy showed up, you'd be in deep shit. I'd make sure of that."

Falco, the beanpole (who had a mean-looking squint), said to Carl: "What's your name?"

Carl: "Why do you need to know that?"

Falco: "Listen, soldier, you looking for trouble?"

Carl mumbled his name, hoping they wouldn't understand him.

Butch, the Fat Man: "And where do you work, Duncan?"

More mumbling: "Headquarters Company."

"I'm going to look you up. Go through your personnel records. See what kind of trouble you've been in. I don't like guys who dick with me."

"Yes, sir."

Falco (raising his voice): "We're not officers. Don't call us sir."

Carl: "I understand."

Falco: "Then understand your way out of here. If we ever find you at this beach again, you're going to be sorry you were ever born."

. . .

Carl told me about his experience with the MPs.

"How come Ken didn't show up?" I asked. "Did he hear you talking?"

"I don't know. This just happened and I haven't spoken to him yet. But I can't think of any other reason."

"Like the MPs said, you're very lucky."

I assumed he would agree with me and sound relieved. But no. "Even if Ken *did* appear, they wouldn't have had anything on us."

According to the version I had just heard, that wasn't how he felt at the time. "Suppose Ken had gotten there early? Suppose he'd been on the bench when you arrived?"

"But he wasn't. And anyway, I probably would have heard the MPs on the beach."

"Maybe you wouldn't have," I warned. "You had a close call. I hope you learned a lesson."

"Don't worry about me!" He sounded almost cocky. "I can take care of myself. I know enough not to go back to that beach. We'll find someplace else."

Obviously, he could see I was upset and we reversed roles. *He* tried to cheer *me* up: "I told you before I'm careful. So stop worrying."

I couldn't think of anything else to say.

Not that he would have heard me anyway.

LAUGHING AT THE H-BOMB

———————— ⚛ ————————

THE ISLAND SEEMED QUIETER WITHOUT TONY AND ESTABROOK AND EDER. AND then Clarence Killebrew arrived to liven up the joint. He was a burly San Francisco construction worker with a bulldog face, and he announced as soon as he settled into Tony's old bed above mine that he had no intention of taking any more shit. Not that anyone asked.

During the next twenty-four hours, he banged on the aluminum walls. He threw books around the room. Not his own—he didn't read—but everyone else's. He emptied all the footlockers and hurled the contents down the hallway and also out the barracks windows (which didn't close). Richter called him a disrupting influence. Berko said he was a human version of the H-bomb.

By popular request, the MPs came for him, put him in handcuffs and threw him in a cell with the same amount of gentleness that he had displayed toward our belongings. I suspect the authorities came to the same conclusion about *him* that the major and the doctor did about me: He was acting that way to get off the island. And maybe he was. But this was not the best method of achieving that goal. As awful as life in the barracks was, it was an improvement over the Eniwetok jail. And that is where he stayed—without anything to throw around in his new quarters. I don't know what happened to Killebrew, but my guess is that he ended up spending twelve months on The Rock outside a cell in addition to the time he spent behind bars.

The next test, Number Ten, had the code name Osage. This was the shot everybody was nervous about: For the second time ever, an H-bomb was going to be dropped from a plane (this time a B-36). Nobody on The Rock could forget that the first one had landed far from its Bikini target, and I didn't know a man who wasn't expecting the fireball in front of us again.

This device was scheduled to detonate much closer to home, on Eniwetok Atoll. Ground zero was supposed to be the island of (what else?) Runit (Yvonne). It was just a few miles from Eniwetok Island, so a miss this time could turn Joint Task Force Seven's headquarters into ground zero.

Osage was an air drop with a burst altitude of seven hundred feet, a proof test of a lightweight low-yield plutonium warhead intended for air defense.

We were lined up as usual, eyes closed. Hoping, if not praying.

The countdown. Five, four, three, two, one, zero. Blast.

And then we waited some more. When the D.V. finally announced that we could open up our eyes, we did. And were almost surprised that the bomb was behind us. This time, practice *did* make perfect. The pilot hit his target.

I felt only silent relief. Berko was more demonstrative: He clapped his hands together. I followed his lead. And then Duncan and Straletti and Richter and Craig and Jason Underwood did the same thing. Seconds later, dozens of other soldiers joined in and a few of us put on our sunglasses.

I noticed Major Maxwell. Hair unruly, food stain on his shirt, mouth twisted into a scowl.

"Stop that!" he shrieked, splattering saliva all over his own chin. "Stop that! This is the army! Remember you're in the army!"

But the grunts were out there watching a mushroom cloud and we were cheering and applauding and laughing our asses off. We weren't going to stop, and there was absolutely nothing the major could do about it.

That afternoon Berko said to me: "Do you realize what we did this morning?"

Always a straight man for him, I replied: "We applauded a pilot who didn't miss his target when he dropped an H-bomb."

"We were *laughing*," he said.

"Yes, we were laughing too," I agreed.

"We were laughing at the H-bomb!" Berko said. "Do you realize that? Now tell me, how often does that happen?"

"Not much."

"It should happen more. This fucking island has taught me something, and I have a hunch it's important. You have to be able to laugh at everything. Even an H-bomb. Otherwise you'll never stop crying."

"You have a point there," I said.

And both of us laughed.

I was always overhearing peculiar conversations in the mess hall line and it happened again the next morning. I was standing behind an army man visiting The Rock for the day. He was stationed on Japtan, home of the giant clams and banana-shaped coconuts, and also the closest inhabited island to Runit. This soldier was telling the man next to him that he backed up into the water during all the Runit blasts.

"I want to be able to tell my grandchildren I was only seven miles from those H-bomb explosions," he said. "Closer than anyone else at the Proving Ground during Operation Redwing."

Naturally, I told Berko what I had heard and he had the same reaction I did. By actually standing in the lagoon when the countdown reached zero, that guy may have made sure he was never going to have any grandchildren to tell.

"You have to laugh," I said.

Berko didn't skip a beat: "Or else you'll never stop crying."

A BETTER MAN

A FEW DAYS LATER I GOT A LETTER FROM TONY. *DEAR FRIEND*, HE BEGAN, THE
first time he had ever called me a "friend." Then he brought me up to
date on his life since he left The Rock.

"Now that I'm off the island, I realize I was much more bothered
by the navy men in the hospital than I thought at the time. Between
those guys and Irene's cancer, I've started to think about things in a
different way. When you and I first met, I didn't want to get involved.
I just wanted to be left alone. I've changed since then, and now it looks
like I'm going full speed ahead in the opposite direction.

"You may find this hard to believe, but I've decided to go to med
school. Dr. Tankeray, who helped Irene recover, is recommending me,
so my chances look pretty good. And best of all, the G.I. Bill is going to
pay for it."

Then he was back again to Life with Father.

"Did I ever mention to you that I went to law school? My father
wanted me to go, so I did. He was P.O.'d when I refused to apply to West

Point, so I figured that for once I'd try to please him. But I hated law school and left after one semester. In my old man's eyes, I was a quitter!

"When I told him about med school, I figured he'd come up with another way to put me down. I half expected him to tell me again that I should have been a lawyer, but he surprised me. He seemed happy about it and even said he was proud of me. I hate to be cynical but I wonder how long *that* will last?

"Irene says he's mellowed—they made up after a long, drunken, teary evening. It turns out that one reason he (and the rest of my family) were so angry at her was because she refused to tell them who Patty's father was. They assumed he was some spic she picked up in a bar for a one-night stand (as my old man so charmingly put it). When he found out the guy was a Korean War hero who was killed in action—*and* Italian—his attitude changed. Doesn't that make you want to puke? In fact, it's pretty outrageous considering my own mom isn't Italian. She's Irish!

"According to Irene, the old man's changed, but I'll wait and see. Maybe he'll surprise me again and we'll end up being friends. But if he's still the same stubborn bastard, I'll keep my distance."

Tony wrote that Irene was happy and healthy for the first time in a long while, and after coming so close to death, she valued life more than ever.

"I can say the same for myself after my own brushes with death— Wilson's bullet and the H-bombs. Looking back, I have to say The Rock was a lot worse than I used to admit, but it did help me get my head on straight. I'm a better man now than I was when I first got to that fucking island.

"There was nothing we could do about the H-bombs or some of the incompetence, but we fought back when we could and we managed to survive. And what's more important than that?

"So hang in there and keep fighting. *Don't* give up!"

I put his letter down and thought about how much we were all changing. And I wondered if maybe I was starting to take Kevin Tonnello seriously.

THE SOUND OF NO CLICKING

INCA, NUMBER ELEVEN, WAS A TWO-HUNDRED-FOOT-HIGH TOWER SHOT ON RU-joru (Pearl) Island, Eniwetok Atoll, and tested a "multi-application boosted tactical nuclear warhead prototype."

The explosion was followed by fallout number four. The clicking was louder and faster than it was during the others, and that meant more radioactive particles assaulting us. Today we were being fried in style.

I sat at my desk and felt too much and nothing at all. At the same time.

I remembered the *Radiological Monitor's Safety Handbook* distributed to us in February. Inside was a list of the four basic methods of decontamination: surface cleaning, surface removal, disposal and natural decay. I decided that morning that I belonged in the fourth category. Natural decay.

I thought about the navy men at the Snakepit and the hospital and wondered if that was the first hint of what might happen to *us* someday. The most common short-term symptoms had not yet afflicted anyone I knew in the army. No loss of hair. No skin lesions. No diarrhea or nausea. But what about the future? Were we being poisoned? Would we bleed internally? Had our genetic code been compromised? Would we get leukemia or some other form of cancer? Would our children (if we ever had them) be born without limbs or internal organs?

I didn't know it then, but one-third of the crew of the USS *Navasota*, at Eniwetok during Redwing, would die of cancer before the age of fifty-five. And similar numbers for the men of the USS *Belle Grove*. And perhaps all the ships, although statistics are not readily available today. Some men were attacked by *slow* bullets that did not reach their targets for years. Others, like Geezer, had a shorter wait.

American Atomic Veterans have had a much higher risk of cancer: a 20 percent higher risk of fatal prostate cancer, a 160 percent higher risk of nasal cancer, a 14 percent higher risk of dying from leukemia. Radiation exposure "significantly increased" the risk of noncancerous diseases, causing heart disease, strokes, pneumonia and liver problems. Radioactive fallout from Cold War nuclear tests caused at least 15,000 cancer deaths in U.S. residents born after 1951 and 20,000 nonfatal cancers—possibly many more. (Sources: *Journal of the American Medical Association*, Radiation Effects Research Foundation in Hiroshima, Centers for Disease Control and Prevention in Atlanta.)

In the year 2000, the Institute of Medicine (part of the National Academy of Sciences) studied the mortality rate of Atomic Veterans and discovered we are up to two and a half times more likely to die of thyroid, bone, prostate, male breast, and nasal cancer, and cancer of the testes.

But some scientists did not have to wait fifty years and examine statistics to understand the damage resulting from these tests. In 1956, British physician Alice Stewart found the first firm evidence that low-level radiation causes cancer in human beings. And not all the radiation on Eniwetok was low-level.

In 1957, Linus Pauling, close friend of Albert Einstein and twice a winner of an unshared Nobel Prize—for Chemistry and for Peace—estimated that ten thousand persons had already died or were dying from leukemia as a result of atomic tests.

Men at the Proving Ground were giving their lives for their country. Without knowing they were doing it.

The statistics are not any different from what I imagined in June 1956. Geezer had left the hospital in a body bag, and it was not much of a leap to assume that other lives would be cut short too. My only questions were: How soon? And would I be one of them?

Then and now, I had no idea who to blame. Who were the bad guys? The military? The Pentagon? The Joint Chiefs of Staff? Joint Task Force Seven? The Atomic Energy Commission? Lewis Strauss? The scientists? The president? The Soviet Union? The Cold War? During the hot wars, it's much easier to figure out who the enemy is. There's "them" and there's "us." I knew who "we" were back then. But who were "they"?

I sat in the depot during fallout number four surrounded by men I didn't know. I had been on The Rock that long. Many of the faces looked familiar, and I knew some of the names, though we didn't have conversations often. I still talked to the old-timers, but I spent the rest of the time inside my shell.

I looked around and saw Whitaker (I think he was from New Mexico) with his hands over his ears.

Billy Byrne typed requisitions.

A redheaded guy was singing.

Rasmusson was praying (he was earning a good income in the barracks renting out porno magazines "with or without jerk-off stains"— with stains was cheaper).

Two men were staring into space. The Kilmer Look. Good old "Rock Disease."

Another two were telling each other dirty jokes and laughing. Suddenly the smile vanished from the face of one of them and he shouted: "This place is shit! What could be worse than an island without women!"

A young gray-haired man was whistling.

Sapinsley couldn't stop coughing. I wondered why. Was he sick? Or just plain nervous?

I listened to the wild clicking and thought about a favorite radio program of mine when I was a child, *Your Hit Parade* (later a television program I liked less). I sat there and made up my own all-time *Eniwetok Hit Parade* with the highlights of the past year. My worst moments on the island: the headaches, the doctor's examination, the exile to the gulag, the bombs exploding in front of us. But I concluded then that the fourth fallout belonged at the top of the list. Number One. I could not remember another time in my life when I felt worse than I did that morning.

I was aware of strange noises coming from my throat. They seemed to be somewhere between laughter and tears. A few of the men looked over at me, but I did not stop. I did not even know if I could. I suspected the sounds were not voluntary.

I thought about Tony's advice to me: *Hang in there and keep fighting. Don't give up. Nothing matters more than surviving!* Those were not words that could help me at a moment I was being cooked alive.

The clicking was sharp and clear through the open windows and continued for many hours. Then there was silence, followed by an all-clear announcement over the loudspeaker. We had permission to open up the windows again.

No one moved.

Permission to open up. That's what I had. I could stop burying my feelings. I was now allowed to let go. I could refrain from censoring my thoughts and controlling my emotions. Which I didn't do very well anyway. I could stop pretending I was not afraid. Which I also didn't do very well.

I had permission to open up. I was free to be me again. Or free to be somebody new. Maybe, like Tony, a different and better person.

No rain and no clicking anymore. I realized then I had survived another day. I could not know what would happen to me in the future, but I was sure about that morning. For the time being, I had survived.

What I experienced next was a strange, quiet, peaceful exhilaration. And at this time and this place, that feeling was as good as it gets.

I didn't have the vaguest idea why, but for some odd reason I was proud of myself. Because in the end I had managed to push away the terrors for a while? Because I did not allow myself to be defeated?

I reflected. And I realized I had made an important discovery that morning. I finally knew that the most beautiful music in the world is the sound of no clicking.

PIECES OF A SOLDIER

CARL CAME UP TO ME IN THE MESS HALL LINE AT BREAKFAST, PALE AND SHAKING. I thought something had happened with Ken. But no, Carl had been taking a breather since the night with the MPs. He wasn't ready yet to see Ken again. But soon. Definitely soon.

"I took an early morning walk along the beach at Oceanview National Park," he explained. "Pieces of a body were lying next to the snail and lobster shells. Part of a face and a torn khaki shirt. And what looked like an arm and an ankle."

"Did you tell anyone?"

He shook his head. "I don't want to get involved with the MPs again."

"It was the sharks," I guessed. "Someone went for a walk in the ocean. I wonder if it was anyone we know."

"It was." Carl's eyes teared up and I waited for him to speak. Finally: "The right side of his face was on the sand. I saw the large brown mole."

Jason Underwood! I was now shaking as much as Carl. I wondered if something in particular had pushed him over the edge. Or was it just general Rock malaise?

I waited in line silently for my powdered eggs, remembering how much Jason Underwood enjoyed them. On this day I didn't even notice if the cooks used the Geiger counter.

By late afternoon, everyone knew what had happened, but I had no idea how or when they found out. I never once heard Jason Underwood's name mentioned. By anyone. In the barracks or the office or anywhere else.

I did see people walk past his room and stop at the door and look inside and stare at his bed and footlocker. Stare at the emptiness. At the space once occupied by a person but now filled only by air.

I did see people whispering. Soundlessly. But otherwise this felt like the same silence that took over the island the first time the H-bomb exploded in front of us.

Everyone had talked about Billy Byrne and the aloha noose, but *that* never threatened us. Billy Byrne didn't succeed. No one wanted to think about Jason Underwood—we were all afraid of being tempted too much.

The next morning, an MP came by and took away all his belongings. Nobody, including me and the MP, said a word.

Only Carl dared to tread on ground that no one else would get near. "It's a horrible way to go," he told me, "but maybe the poor guy is better off. He got it over with quickly."

"I hope you're not considering that yourself," I said, immediately concerned.

"I didn't say that."

But he didn't need to. "Learn a lesson from Billy Byrne," I told him. "He was lucky Tony found him in time."

"I guess so." He was talking in a monotone.

"He's happy today. If you don't believe me, ask *him* if he'd rather be alive or dead right now." Happy because the other men accepted him. Or pretended to. Though he chose a risky way of achieving that goal.

Carl: "For me, the worst moment of every day is the first second after I wake up in the morning. When I'm asleep, I forget where I am, but as soon as I open up my eyes I remember, and I have to adjust all over again. As everyone says on The Rock, it's all downhill from there."

"I got a letter from Tony," I told him. "And you know what he said? The Rock plus Irene's cancer makes them both value life more than ever. 'Just hang in there,' he told me. 'Surviving is what it's all about.' "

"Is that what he said?"

I nodded.

"Do you think he knows anything?"

I nodded again.

When I saw Carl that evening, his black mood was gone. Or at least it had turned into a light gray.

Did Tony have anything to do with it? Did I? I wanted to think so.

"I stopped by the repair shop this afternoon," he told me.

So now I knew the answer. It wasn't either of us. It was Superman.

"Ken has left The Rock," Carl said. "His twelve months were up."

Why didn't Carl look devastated?

"And he never bothered to say good-bye," Carl told me.

"Maybe he was too upset by the MPs. He probably heard your conversation and got scared. So he left The Rock without saying anything."

"You're just trying to make me feel better," Carl said.

"That's true. I don't want you to take a walk in the ocean."

Tony had said to me once that the worst mistake you can make on The Rock is to "feel sorry for yourself." That was The Original Tony. Before he met the navy men in the hospital. Before he became a new and better person back in the States. I often thought about all three Tonys.

Today, Carl was "feeling sorry for himself," and that could have disastrous consequences.

Carl: "Ken left *before* my night with the MPs at Oceanview National Park. He didn't show up because he had already left The Rock."

I was surprised. And more surprised that Carl didn't look deeply depressed as he was speaking.

"Maybe I was lucky," Carl said.

"You think so?"

"I don't know for sure, but I think so. Maybe everything turned out for the best."

I assumed he was just putting on a brave front. Which was okay. A million percent better than being despondent.

Carl: "I was going to see Ken in the States but now I doubt if I will. And I may be better off. I'm free to start over again when I get home. Whatever that means. I can spend some time adjusting and thinking about the direction I want my life to go in."

"Whatever that means," I said.

"I mean, I don't know who I am anymore, and it's about time I found out."

"So is there something to celebrate?" I asked. "If there is, maybe we should stop by the Snakepit tonight and give Hula and Gizmo and Buddy a few pretzels."

"And I might even have a beer myself," he said. "I'm beginning to think a little drink now and then isn't such a bad idea."

And I held up my arm, an imaginary glass in my fingers, and proposed a silent toast to both of us. And to the dogs.

THE CHOICE

A FEW DAYS LATER, CAPTAIN WEISS TOLD ME I HAD DONE AN OUTSTANDING JOB at the depot. I was a private first class, and he wanted to reward me with a promotion.

I looked at him with the familiar Eniwetok blank expression and politely thanked him. He seemed almost hurt that I didn't respond with more enthusiasm, so I tried to rev myself up and sound a little more grateful.

I must have failed because he went on to tell me I had a choice. I didn't have to accept the promotion. I could remain a plain old PFC but leave The Rock (AND the army) one month early. Which meant I would depart from Eniwetok in less than ten days.

Captain Weiss asked me to consider the two alternatives carefully. I inspected his face and could not find even a trace of a smile. I didn't see how it was possible, but he was serious. Did he believe the promotion would be important to this atomic draftee?

He advised me to take my time and think about it, but, impulsive individual that I am, the amount of time I took can be measured in fractions of a second. I estimate two nanoseconds.

Did I display excitement or even feel it? Of course not. I was just too numb.

I was given a Certificate of Participation in Operation Redwing. On this piece of paper, the largest word is "Greetings," the same one that appeared on my original draft notice. Underneath, it says "Know Ye: We the undersigned do hereby certify that Michael Harris participated in Operation Redwing." The words "Operation Redwing" are printed on the side of an Indian teepee, which also has pictures of two birds, a sun, a moon, a star and (can it be?) a swastika. Underneath the teepee it says "Eniwetok."

Also on this certificate, there are:

1. An Indian sitting on a log, weaving a rectangular rug that has U.S. ARMY printed on it in capital letters.

2. Three airplanes.

3. One boat.

4. A palm tree (with no woman behind it).

5. A mushroom cloud.

6. And two pieces of rope that look suspiciously like nooses to me.

In the bottom right-hand corner are the printed signatures of three navy admirals, one air force general, one army general and the scientific director (presumably a civilian).

I also received two letters of a more personal nature: Letters of Commendation. The first was written by Captain Weiss but was over the signature of the higher-ranking Major Vanish. It says:

"On the eve of your departure from Eniwetok, Marshall Islands (Pacific Proving Ground), I wish to express my appreciation for your excellent performance of duty as Requisition Clerk, Depot Supply Office, Task Group 7.2.

"During your tenure you displayed initiative and definite clerical organizational ability. The work performed by you with regard to the requisitioning of supplies and equipment for all task groups and arrangement of files, follow up and maintaining up-to-date status on Major Items Requisitions from JTF-Seven was of material benefit and aid to the Depot in accomplishing its mission. The rank held by you was far below the responsibilities of your position and I desire to commend you for the manner in which you bridged the gap.

"All of the personnel join me in wishing you success in your civilian ventures upon your honorable discharge from the Army of the United States."

The second letter, written by my company commander, says: "It is a pleasure to note the attached letter of commendation (over Major Vanish's signature) and to add my approval. Your professional skill and willing devotion to duty have been consistently characteristic of your service in this organization. I have directed that a copy of this correspondence be placed in your field military 201 file."

Two nice letters but I particularly appreciated the one written by Captain Weiss because we knew each other so well. I always liked him and I was grateful for his rescue mission at the Snakepit.

And I ended up being the *soldier* who was different. I doubt if any other veterans of the Eniwetok battleground were praised in writing for "definite clerical organizational ability."

Five days to go, but Joint Task Force Seven was not finished with me yet. I was going to get *my* farewell present.

Number Twelve, Dakota, was the second barge shot in Operation Redwing, and ground zero was the same as the first: the Flathead test site, five thousand feet off Yurochi (Dog) Island, Bikini Atoll lagoon.

After the early morning march in single file, we waited in formation for the countdown, and I wondered what was in store for me today.

I thought about Number Ten. Laughing at the H-bomb. Was that a blueprint for my future?

Maybe Berko was right. In order to survive, maybe it *was* important to be able to laugh at everything. At least for me. To laugh at myself. At life. At death. At nuclear explosions. At a ludicrous major who seemed intent on killing us all. Maybe that was the only way to keep away the tears.

I remembered a childhood when I couldn't stop crying. When kids taunted me for not having a mother, only a German "baby nurse." I was left out and lonely and never found a way to fight back. I couldn't look at the craziness around me then and see it for what it was.

But now, after months of training in the South Pacific, I was beginning to make progress. I could look at my one-square-mile world and see how absurd it was. I was learning how to laugh. Maybe the island had made me certifiable, but at least I had discovered a way of dealing with the clowns.

The countdown began for the last bomb I would ever see, hear and feel, and I remembered the bombs of my childhood. During World War II, I had the same nightmare many times a week: bombs exploding around me. In the dreams, I was with Fraulein in *her* city, Bremerhaven, Germany, and the two of us were alone and huddled together in the dark. Holding on tightly and taking care of each other. And every evening we succeeded in staying together and staying alive.

In my adult anger, I had forgotten how much I needed Fraulein when I was a child. I prepared to watch my last mushroom cloud and I remembered the ways she had saved my life. She was the only one who ever asked me what I did during the day when I came home from grade school. She was a tutor of sorts, helping me learn the multiplication tables as we strolled together through Central Park.

In my childhood dreams, Fraulein and I were clinging to each other for protection and survival. Not far from the truth. The child I used to be was all she ever had, and she was the only mother I ever knew. She cared for me when there was no one else. And if she had not stopped my father from ignoring me, I might never have had a second parent. With that conversation she saved my life again. And maybe she ended her own by losing me.

On that morning on Eniwetok, I finally realized that what she did TO me paled compared to what she did FOR me. She and I were bound together, for better and for worse. It was too late for me to help her, but not too late for me to understand how much she had helped me. I realized I would never have made it without her. Fraulein was the first person to give me survival lessons.

Poor Fraulein. During World War II, when we were together, strangers in New York threatened her when they realized she was German. And at the same time, her family in Bremerhaven really *was* being bombed. She was as unhappy and isolated as I was.

As a child, I dreamed about bombs. As an adult, I looked at bombs and felt sorry for Fraulein. Not just for myself. And the new compassion was something good that came out of that year.

I opened my eyes and watched the cloud rise to a height of 81,000 feet, with a diameter at stabilization of 93,000 feet. And I saw it move in three directions: the upper portion traveled west-northwest; the middle, east-northeast; the bottom and stem, northwest. The upper umbrella extended to Eniwetok Island with what JTF7 described as "patches" of radioactive material.

I learned later that Dakota was a success story for the army. The W-28 small-diameter, lightweight ("Class-D") thermonuclear weapon design became the most versatile and widely used ever adopted by the United States, fielded in five models with twenty variants. The W-28 was in use from 1958 to 1990 (with the last one dismantled in September 1991).

Dakota was a success for me too.

I don't remember much that happened during the next five days while I waited to leave. I was "shook." I had always wondered what went on inside the heads of the "shook" men who were on their way out, and I learned the answer: Nothing. My mind was totally blank. I didn't even think about home. I had imagined I would be ecstatic when I was about to depart, but instead I was totally zonked. Like the other men I had seen go before me, I was there but not there, myself but not me.

But I do remember that when the plane took off I was laughing. Not that this was any great accomplishment considering that my Magic Number was now zero, but it seemed important to me at the time.

And I remember that when I looked down at The Rock and watched it get smaller and smaller, I said to myself (proudly): I've survived.

I was certain then I was going to survive in the future, no matter where I was, no matter what surprises the world had in store for me.

I had absolutely no rational reason for believing that, but it turned out to be true.

EPILOGUE

Certificate of participation

THE LAST FIVE TESTS

I FOUND OUT ABOUT THE LAST FIVE TESTS IN LETTERS FROM BERKO AND CARL. And I corroborated what they told me in official government documents on Operation Redwing, once secret, now declassified.

Mohawk (13) was a three-hundred-foot-high tower shot on Eberiru (Ruby) Island, Eniwetok Atoll. Berko, immersed in the new baseball season, described the shot as "strictly Minor League stuff. Just one hour of clicking."

Ground zero for Apache (14) was the Ivy Mike crater on Eniwetok Atoll. Carl wrote: "The fallout was heavy." Berko: "We're not in the Minor Leagues anymore."

Navajo (15), a Bikini barge shot, had a huge yield of 4.5 megatons, dwarfing Cherokee, the previous record-holder with a measly 3.8. The press had colorfully referred to Cherokee as "the monster bomb," but as Berko put it, "Yesterday's champion is today's has-been."

Tewa (16) exploded ten days later and had an even higher yield of 5 megatons, 11 percent more than Navajo. "Less than two weeks have passed," Berko wrote, "and already a new champion has been crowned!"

Tewa had a fission yield of 87 percent, the highest known of any U.S. thermonuclear test, making it the "dirtiest" bomb ever. But size and fission yield were the least of it. Tewa was the deadliest Redwing test by far, and, like Castle Bravo, the destructiveness was unexpected and due to a "shift" in the wind.

Eniwetok was hit by very heavy fallout that lasted for *days*, and Carl and Berko (and the rest of the men) were exposed to seven and a half times more radiation than they received from all the other sixteen tests combined. After I read their letters, I realized my choice might not have been only between an early departure and a promotion but between a long life and a premature death.

The Bikini barge, site of ground zero, turned into a burning ball of fire and jumped up into the air alongside the mushroom cloud. After the blast, millions of dead fish floated on the surface for miles and miles alongside tens of thousands of dead birds, scooped up by live sharks and barracuda (fusion cuisine, aquatic style). Fish also inhabited the tops of coconut palms that Tewa had not blasted apart.

Huron (17) was the final shot and took place the morning after Tewa. Eniwetok was still receiving heavy fallout from the Tewa cloud, so there is some doubt about how much Huron added to the continuing radioactivity.

Carl wrote: "Tewa was so powerful it lit up the sky in Hawaii, over 2,000 miles away. People there thought the sun was rising."

The rest of his letter was personal stuff. He said Penny had broken up with his "friend" Keith and wanted to get back together with him. "I'm beginning to think that's possible. I never did return the engagement ring to the PX. Maybe I knew all along I'd need it. Richter says there are no accidents. At any rate, thinking about Penny has helped me get through these final tests."

Berko was more specific about what they were getting through.

"Stop the presses! We're not allowed to swim in the lagoon anymore! As soon as I found out, I got worried the three-eyed fish would get lonely without us paddling around next to them. So I decided to cheer them up and threw them the entire box of cookies I got today from my mother. I hope the fish end up as fat and content as the Brooklyn pigeons.

"But the main reason I'm writing is because I've got a couple of stories for you that belong in our favorite category: You have to laugh or you'll never stop crying.

"The first involves the new swimming regulation. When do you think JTF7 decided it's not safe to go in the lagoon? This morning, right after Huron, when Operation Redwing was over! No problem with our going into the water during all the explosions and all the fallouts—it only became dangerous the moment the tests ended!

"The second story is sadder and funnier. Before Redwing started, JTF7 decided it would be unsafe to expose men on The Rock to radiation levels higher than 3.9 roentgens. That was exceeded during the Tewa fallout, and three ships—the *Curtiss*, the *Ainsworth* and the *Knudson*—were rushed to Eniwetok from Bikini to evacuate personnel. But all the ships were ordered back to Bikini while they were still en route because the evacuation turned out to be unnecessary. Why? JTF7 simply raised the allowable dosage to 7 roentgens. By increasing the maximum permissible exposure, JTF7 immediately made Eniwetok safe for everyone here.

"I'm going to have to end my letter now. I'm laughing so hard I can't write anymore.

"Your friend, Berko."

AFTER THE ROCK

———— ⚛ ————

I FLEW AWAY FROM THE CUCKOO'S NEST AND LIVED HAPPILY EVER AFTER. TRUE OR false?

True *and* false.

Like the other men I lived with on The Rock, I imagined that when I returned to "civilization," everything would be as good as it had been before and probably much better. But the isolation played tricks on our memories. We substituted new fantasies for the old realities, and ended up with inaccurate pictures of the world we left behind. As a result, many of us forgot how to relate to people. Especially to women, as I found out quickly.

On my way back to New York, I had a one-day layover in Honolulu and met a very nice Hawaiian girl. We went for a romantic evening walk on Waikiki and I took her in my arms and I was about to kiss her when I opened my big mouth. "For the past twelve months," I told her, "I've been on an island with only men. I haven't kissed a woman in a year." She responded to my announcement with terror and sprinted down the beach away from me as fast as she could.

That was the beginning of the relearning process for me. I never again made that particular mistake, but there were plenty of others. Just as stroke patients often need to learn how to walk and talk again, I had to relearn what to say and how to behave. Whatever social skills I had acquired before the army were gone, and I had a tough time getting a date for Saturday night. The Rock had turned me into an awkward adolescent all over again. It took a while but I made progress, and eventually there were new Nancys, attractive and appealing women who mattered to me, if only for the moment.

I had laughed at the compliment to my clerical and organizational skills, which I considered my contribution to the war effort: I filed my way to victory. And yet my first civilian job was much less challenging. I delivered mail at CBS for forty dollars a week. But it was a start. This time around I agreed to a promotion from private first class (I became assistant photo editor), and before too long other promotions followed. Eventually I worked my way up to the network equivalent of—what? Major? Colonel? I was a public relations executive at CBS Television for many years.

I was especially close to Ed Sullivan, a sort of mentor to me. He was a very smart man who acted intuitively and rarely explained why he made his decisions (even to the staff of his own program). I was an exception, and I heard and learned and I was grateful for the education. We had one brief fallout when he felt I betrayed him by writing his "unauthorized" biography. But he ended up promoting the book and appearing with me on television talk shows. Thanks in great part to his help, *Always on Sunday* was a bestseller.

My health? It's been good and so has my eyesight. For years I had chronic conjunctivitis and learned not long ago (from recently declassified documents) that so did other Atomic Veterans. But my conjunctivitis is not chronic anymore and hasn't bothered me in years. I also have glaucoma, an eye disease that can cause blindness, but with drops and surgery I have kept the disease in check, and with glasses I have 20/20 vision.

I try not to think about The Rock but I still have recurrent night-

262 · THE ATOMIC TIMES

mares. I dream about bombs, just as I did in my childhood, though now all the explosions are nuclear. For me, surviving has been easier than forgetting, and maybe that's good.

The Happiest Ever After part began with Ruth. On March 12, 1970, at 7:13 P.M.

I knew her forever the moment we met. And she knew me just as long. Right away we were the closest of friends and much, much more. Love at first instant and every instant after that.

So *this* is what it was all about. I survived the obstacle course and found the reward. The ring I placed on Ruth's finger came from the pot of gold at the end of the nuclear rainbow. And loneliness, at last, was banished for good.

We knew at once we would never spend even one night apart.

And we never have.

ABOUT THE AUTHOR

MICHAEL HARRIS began writing *The Atomic Times* in 1955, when he was an army draftee stationed on Eniwetok, and finished fifty years later. In between, he married novelist Ruth Harris (in 1970) and spent years as a public relations executive at CBS Television, eleven of them on the staff of *The Ed Sullivan Show*. In addition to welcoming the Beatles at the airport on their first trip to the United States, he is the author of *Always on Sunday*, the bestselling (and unauthorized) biography of Ed Sullivan.

ABOUT THE TYPE

This book was set in Photina, a typeface designed by José Mendoza in 1971. It is a very elegant design with high legibility, and its close character fit has made it a popular choice for use in quality magazines and art gallery publications.